Prayers

by
Judith Hannemann
Illustrations by Christine Simoneau Hales

authorHOUSE®

AuthorHouse™
1663 Liberty Drive, Suite 200
Bloomington, IN 47403
www.authorhouse.com
Phone: 1-800-839-8640

First published by AuthorHouse 2/13/2008

ISBN: 978-1-4343-1093-4 (hc)
ISBN: 978-1-4343-1094-1 (sc)

Library of Congress Control Number: 2007904441

Printed in the United States of America
Bloomington, Indiana

This book is printed on acid-free paper.

Scriptures cited are from:

Dedicated to Jake

Beloved husband. Traveling companion in the Kingdom.

For the Reader

Come, Holy Spirit of Prayer,

In Your holy sweetness, be with the dear person who opens these pages of prayer.

Even as Your grace precedes prayer, precede every word, sentence, punctuation, and paragraph of this book. May those who read herein find encouragement and refreshed faithfulness.

Honor the reader's heart with courage in believing all prayer is answered.

In Your mercy, honor my prayer for the reader to experience Your grace in knowing he or she is loved by God and by me.

The words of this request are offered in the Name of the Lord Jesus Christ,

Whose sweet Spirit You are.

Amen.

Welcome, Holy Spirit, to these pages.

REQUESTS TO GOD

WHATEVER YOU ASK FOR IN PRAYER, BELIEVE THAT YOU HAVE RECEIVED IT. AND IT WILL BE YOURS.

MARK 11:24

Traveling

May God grant to you a Bethel heart in your journey towards Him. Where the stones of disappointment, exhaustion and pain are your pillows, may you be able to rest in Him. And may your soul see it is surrounded by angels and your needs ascend to Heaven on a ladder of grace.

Whatsoever place you are in right now in your life, may you hear El Shaddai saying He is with you and will keep you wherever you go and will always bring you back to Him.

Whatsoever place you are in right now in your life, may you say with Jacob, "Surely the Lord is in this place and I did not know it."

This is my prayer for you.

Amen.

Genesis 28:10-18 (RSV)

God our Friend

Lord God Almighty,

As if it were not enough that You created us, gave each of us life, You have also befriended us. You are the friend our hearts have always longed for; a trusted confidante of our sorrows, a steadfast helper in our times of need, a divine Lover pursuing and romancing our souls. You gave us Your Son Jesus Christ that we might drink deeply of His Living Water and be forgiven, refreshed, reconciled to You. You heal our illnesses and hurts; You grant justice to the oppressed; You shower Your mercy upon the just and the unjust; You give us Your wisdom through the counsel of the Holy Spirit.

Almighty God. Holy God. Powerful God. Merciful God. Indeed, God, our Friend.

We bless You and we thank You for who You are. God our Friend.

Amen.

Prov. 17:17 (NIV)

Teach Us to Walk

Lord Jesus,

Teach us to walk as You did. Forgive us that we tarry over our sins, fumble for direction and open inappropriate doors instead of the door to our hearts where You stand knocking. We would retrace our steps into the past where we mistake the familiar and the secure for peace.

Teach us to walk as You did. Errant students of Your grace as we are, we shall need You beside us as we grope forward into the will of the Father. Come, now, Savior, walk beside us that Your strength might sustain us. According to Your Word, we know that we are in You if we walk as you did.

Comfort and direct us in each step of the walk among broken individuals and institutions, broken trust and hope.

O Savior, teach us to walk as You did.

Amen.

1 John 2:6 (RSV)

Nets

And immediately they left their nets and followed Him.
Mark 1:18 (RSV)

May you leave the distractions and doubts and discouragements woven around your heart and follow Him.

May you leave the sin entangling you.

May you recognize Jesus walking along the shore of your day as you are mending nets of sorrows, hurts and memories.

May you leave repairing the past to follow Him who makes all things new.

Please accept my prayer for you, Beloved Friend, and pray for me that together our response to Jesus might be immediate.

Amen.

Journey of Joy

May you know all the anointing of the Holy Spirit in His fruit of joy. May you feel closer to your God, your exceeding joy, each time you approach His altar to lay down your life for Jesus. May you feel anew each day the joy of your salvation in remembering your sins are forgiven.

May you be free and spontaneous to make a joyful noise to the Lord as you worship. May you experience the fullness of joy in His presence when you pray and read His Word. And may you so love righteousness and hate wickedness that your God will anoint you with the oil of joy.

May our Blessed Savior, the Lord of Joy, walk with you as you travel towards the heart of God. This is my prayer for you.

Amen.

John 15:11

Holy Hearing

May the grace of a spiritual ear be your gift from God.

May you have an ear to hear, to absorb and to follow Holy Scripture.

May you have an ear to listen with attention to the Holy Spirit. May you have an ear to His promptings for good works and a holy ordered life.

May you have an ear to hear the cry of the poor, the sick and the bereaved.

May you have an ear to hear you are loved by God.

May you and I share the Gospel of this love with all we meet.

Thanks be to God who has an ear for our prayers.

Amen.

Rev.2:17

Hungry Hearing

I will listen to what God the Lord will speak, for He will
speak peace to His people, to His saints, to those who turn to Him in
their hearts.
Psalm 85:8(RSV)

Almighty God,

In Your mercy, grant us ears to listen to You. So inform our hearts
that our wills might hear You amid the daily din overwhelming our
lives. Give us the ears to hear Your guidance and Your love for us in
Holy Scripture, in prayers and in worship.

Your people, Your saints, hunger to hear the peace You will speak
if we will but listen. Answer our prayer that we might the more follow
Your Son, the Lord Jesus Christ, who admonished us to have ears to
hear.

Amen.

Houseguests

Dear Sister,

May grace strengthen you to love God and keep His Word. May your first awakening thought each morning be of God's love for you.

May the Holy Spirit tidy your heart to prepare for, welcome and serve Jesus in all your tasks and troubles.

May the Father, Son and Holy Spirit show their love for you by accepting your hospitality. May you know they are seated at every meal, present in every room, appreciating every effort of your womanly homemaker's heart. May your earthly home and mine be so blessed with Heavenly Houseguests.

Amen.

John 14:23

An Upper Room Heart

May your heart be a large guest room where Jesus is welcome and at home. Clean, bright, warm.

May it be furnished with comfort and not bedraggled dreams, old hurts and angers, sins of others, unforgiveness.

May Jesus feed you Himself, the Bread Come Down from Heaven and the Cup of Salvation.

May you allow Him to wash and dry your feet and your sins. May you know the joy of His teaching and His praying for you, as He does in Heaven.

Sister, be strengthened in readying your upper room heart for your Heavenly Houseguest, the Lord Jesus. Please also pray for me.

Amen.

Mark 14:14-15

Sheltering Love

May you choose to dwell in the shelter of the Most High where you can know deliverance, safe refuge, health and freedom from fear.

May your spirit sense the presence of angels guarding you in all your ways. May their care prevent you from choosing sin stumbling stones over the love of God.

May you hold onto God in such love that you will experience His protection and rescue in the struggles now engaging your life. May you apprehend His honor and salvation because you love Him.

Be blessed by my prayer rendering of Psalm 91 for you, and likewise please remember me in your prayers.

Amen.

Breakfast Companion

Just as day was breaking, Jesus stood on the beach;
John 21:4(RSV)

May the Risen Christ stand on the shore of your day.

May you experience anew His Presence each morning, especially the mornings when the nets of your life are empty.

May the eyes of your soul recognize and respond in joy, "It is the Lord!"

Nourished by His Risen Presence, may you begin your day by telling Him, "Lord, you know I love you."

May you follow your Beloved Breakfast Companion, the Lord Jesus Christ, in whose Name I pray for you.

Amen.

Wilderness Exit

Who is that coming up from the wilderness, leaning on her beloved?
Songs 8:5 (RSV)

Dear Sister,

Whatever is your wilderness as your read these words, be it sorrow for loved ones, grief, ill-health, loneliness, depression, memories, vanquished hopes or destroyed dreams, the Lord invites you to lean on Him. He understands the wilderness of women. May you learn to lean and come up from the wilderness to higher ground in Him. May you know you are loved by Him.

May your heart respond to the tenderness of this Scripture and the intent of my prayer for you.

Amen.

Divine Direction

In all the distractions and discouragements of your day, may the Lord direct your heart.

May the Divine Director reveal His great love for you. May you show and share that love with all persons in your life.

May the Divine Director pave the way in your relationships, events, trials and sorrows.

May the Divine Director increase your joy at the prospect of His Returning.

May you be blessed by the words and intent of this prayer and likewise pray for me.

Amen.

2 Thes. 3:5

A Daniel Blessing for you

May an angel of God touch you and strengthen you. As did Daniel, may you know you are greatly beloved.

May all your fear be replaced by peace.

May you be strong and of good courage.

May you know from the first day you set your mind to understand and humbled yourself before your God, your prayers, the words of your heart, have been heard by God.

Please pray for me to be likewise blessed.

Amen.

Dan. l0:10-19

Emmaus Travel

May an Emmaus heart be your gift from God.

May you know with certainty of soul the Risen Christ walks with you on your particular road.

May you ask Him to stay with you no matter how far gone time, relationships and events in your life.

May He be known to you in the Breaking of Bread each time you approach the Holy Communion table.

May your heart burn within you as He opens the Scriptures to your understanding.

May you accept this prayer and go forth with an Emmaus heart.

Please pray for me, a fellow traveler along the road.

Amen.

Luke 24:13-32

An Achor Reminder

As the Lord your God promised to Israel, His betrothed, so does He to you.

He will revive your present wilderness and speak comfortably to your heart when other voices call you away from Him.

He will give you your vineyards of fruitfulness and productivity in Him.

Your present wilderness will become a door of hope where you will sing and renew the strength of your youth.

The Lord your god will marry your heart with His wedding gifts of righteousness and justice, loving kindness and mercy. Sister, be reminded of His promise and also remind me.

Amen.

Hos. 2:14-20

Cherith Place

And after a while the brook dried up,...
I Kings 17:7(RSV)

Dear friend in the faith,

When you are hiding in a Cherith place and the brook of God's blessings seems dried up, may you be refreshed by the Living Water of Jesus Christ. May you have the courage to come to Him and to drink His strength. May you experience such an astonishment of grace that rivers of Living Water will flow out of your heart. May every prayer I have prayed for you be granted by the generous mercy of God. This is my Cherith prayer for you.

Amen.

Commendation

And now I commend you to God and to the word of His grace,...
Acts 20:32 (RSV)

Grace to remember the Cross is waiting to take your pain and sorrow.

Grace to love mercy enough to extend it to all the people in your life.

Grace to persevere in prayer.

Grace to forgive when it seems impossible.

Grace to accept healing of your past by the One who makes all things new.

Grace to be passionate for your Savior, the Lord Jesus Christ, in whose name I pray for you, because it is well that the heart be strengthened by grace.

Amen.

A Bartimaeus Prayer for You

Be not silenced when you cry out in your present darkness, "'Jesus, Son of David, have mercy on me." Wherever you wait, weep, search, question, despair, cry out again.

He who is Light will stop near you.

Hear His summons. Take courage. Arise. Cast aside the cloak of doubt. Hear Him say, "Go your way; your faith has made you well."

May you receive the restored sight of faithfulness in all the blind spots of your life and your heart. May you then follow Him along the road. This is my prayer for you.

Amen.

Mark 10:46-52 (RSV)

Divine Delight

Take delight in the Lord, and He will give you
the desires of your heart.
Psalm 37:4 (RSV)

May you lay up the Word of God in your heart.

May you keep His testimonies and seek Him with your whole heart. May you hear God wooing you, His beloved, His fair one He beckons come away.

May you repent your sins and find refuge in the pierced heart of Jesus.

May whatsoever you suffer purify your heart to see God.

May His Holy Spirit transform your prayers to God's will for you and your loved ones.

May your heart burn within you as the Risen Christ talks to you and opens the Scripture to you on your own road to Emmaus.

May you be glad in the Lord, shout for joy, and be upright in heart. This is my prayer for you, dear one in the household of faith.

Amen.

Requests to God

Sacred Sight

"Sir, we wish to see Jesus."
John 12:21 (RSV)

May you see Jesus in all the tasks, discouragements, struggles and joys of your day.

May you see Jesus with new and fresh eyes in Holy Scripture. May you see Jesus beside you in prayer, even prayer seeming not heard nor answered.

May you see Jesus in the people He has placed in your life for joy or for sorrow.

May you know the Father honors your every attempt to serve and follow Jesus.

This is my prayer for you, dear seer.

Amen.

Doorway

A door standing open in Heaven.
Rev. 4: 1 (NIV)

May such a door swing open for you, as it did for John, imprisoned on Patmos.

May you experience this glimpse of grace in your own everyday shackles of struggle, sorrow or sickness. May you hear the voice of Him who is seated on the throne. May your voice give blessing and glory and might forever and ever to Him who sits upon the throne. May you find, child of God, renewed purpose and strength to the praise of His glory in your own personal prison.

May you be blessed by the reading of this prayer for you.

Amen.

Requests to God

Happy Birthday

May you be strong to leave your Egypt and enter a new land and a new year in your life.

May you remember it will be a land and a year of hills and valleys, of high and good places and low and dark times in your life.

May God's grace water your hills and your valleys with the rain of Heaven.

May you remember the Lord God cares for you in your new year land, and His eyes are always upon you.

May the Lord Jesus Christ, the Alpha and the Omega, the First and the Last, journey with you on the first as on the last day of this new year land you are entering.

Amen.

Deut. 11:8-12

Go

Thomas, called the twin, said to his fellow disciples,
"Let us also go that we may die with him."
John 11: 16 (RSV)

Lord Jesus Christ,

With Thomas and the disciples, let us also go into whatever You have in store for us. Let us also go to see in our hearts the raising of Lazarus that we might die to self. Let us also go to the unbeliever with the Word of Your salvation. Let us also go to the sick with the assurance You are no stranger to pain and suffering. Let us also go to the elderly with the news You are waiting for them with the porch light on in eternity. Let us also go to the homeless, the addicted, the lonely for whom You died.

Mercifully strengthen us with Your Holy Spirit that we might hear Your call to us and also go.

Amen.

Broom Tree Blessing

Dear One in Jesus,

When you are in a wilderness time, weary under a broom tree of discouragement, may an angel of the Lord awaken your soul and summon you to arise and eat.

May you eat the Bread of Heaven and drink the Living Water that He might satisfy all the hunger and thirst of your life.

Your Savior knows the journey is too great for you. He walks along beside you.

He who has called you into the Kingdom will equip you for traveling towards the heart of God. May you go on in the strength of His grace.

    Amen.

    I Kings 19:7

Choices

May you choose Life. May all your choices, important and trivial, sacred and secular be based on a heart for God.

May you choose to hear the voice of the Lord your God, and then choose to obey it.

May you love God enough to refuse worship and service to the cultural calling of gods of self.

May you have the strength to cling to the Lord your God and follow His commandments, even when the following is dark and difficult.

May you find strength in the closeness of God's word in your mouth, mind and heart. And may you remember me in prayer that I also choose Life.

Amen.

Deut. 30: 11-20

Morning Star

May the Morning Star rise in your heart each day.

May the Lord Jesus Christ illuminate all the dark places in your heart and mind.

May the Morning Star shine into all your struggles with sin, discouragement and grief.

May the Morning Star brighten all your relationships with His wisdom and compassion.

May the Morning Star rise in knowledge of His great love for you.

May you go forth each morning with the incandescence of God.

Please pray for me as I do for you.

Amen.

2 Peter 1:19

The Feminine

Lord Jesus,

All praise to You for seeing into the hearts of women.

All praise to You for blessing their emotions with kindness and forgiveness.

In person or in parable, You were gentle and honored women:

- an anxious and overwhelmed hostess.
      (Luke 10:38-42)

- a widow helpless before a corrupt judge
      (Luke 18: 1-8)

- a repentant woman who wept over your feet
      (Luke 7:36-50)

- a bereaved widow at the funeral of her son
      (Luke 7:13)

- healed and delivered women who traveled with generous women to cook and launder and care for You
      (Luke 8:1-3)

- a good cook
      (Matt. 13:33)

- a woman with a gynecological problem
      (Luke 8:43-48)

- a dying little girl
      (Luke 8:50-56)

- a woman on death row when having an affair led to adultery
      (John 8:3-11)

- a woman in the pain of labor and the joy childbirth
      (John 16:21)

- a desperate mother seeking deliverance for her daughter
      (Matt 15:21-28)

Requests to God

- a mouthy and worldly woman who was thirsty
  (John 4:7-26)

- an impoverished widow with the right priorities of giving
  (Luke 21:1-4)

- women who wept for Your suffering ,unknowing what tragedy and suffering awaited them
  (Luke 23:27-31)

- Your own mother who gave You physical life in birth and stood watching You die
  (John 19:25-27)

- heartbroken and courageous women who came to anoint Your body for burial
  (Matt 28:1-10)

- a grieving and obedient woman at Your tomb
  (John 20:11-18)

Man of Sorrows, thank You for understanding their sorrows and ours.

Mercifully enable us to speak Your message of Love and Salvation to our gender, lost as it is on a turbulent contemporary ocean of denial, despair and deception about the femininity You created.

Thank You, Jesus.

Amen.

Samuel Blessings

Three blessings I ask for you from a most merciful and generous Lord:

When day's lamp is turned off and night's sleep is upon you, may your spirit be quieted to hear God's call.

May you recognize His voice and His love above the distractions and din of everyday and welcome Him by replying, "Speak, here I am"...

"Speak, Lord, for your servant hears".

May the Holy Spirit give you awakened clarity to accept truth and respond, as did Eli, "It is the Lord, let Him do what seems good to Him."

Please likewise pray for me to hear and accept God's truth.

Amen.

1 Sam 3:3-10 (RSV)

Equipment

May the God of peace ... equip you with
everything good for doing His will.
Heb.13:20-21 (NIV)

Good health and strength for your work.

Good judgment in all matters given under your authority in the household of God.

Good relationships and friends to share joy with you.

Good home and family life of order and peacefulness.

Good times of refreshment in prayer and worship.

Good understanding of the Gospel and its message of your salvation.

A good heart for sharing the Gospel of Your Savior, the Lord Jesus Christ, in whose name I pray this blessing for you.

Amen.

Corrective Vision

Blessed are the pure in heart, for they will see God.
Mt 5:8 (NIV)

Dearest Lord Jesus,

Mercifully strengthen us to bring our hearts before You for cleansing purity. There in Your Presence, minister holy transformation to our hearts in the decisions, relationships and activities of our daily round. In You alone is the strength to be what You ask of us. We hunger for the blessed happiness You promise.

By the working of Your Holy Spirit, build our hearts into homes for Your truth, then send us forth with pure hearts and renewed vision to share the message of Your love and salvation with all persons we greet.

Thank You, Dear Savior.

Amen.

Requests to God

Wilderness Praying

But He withdrew to the wilderness and prayed.
Luke 5:16 (RSV)

Blessed Lord Jesus,

You were also in the wilderness and there you prayed.

Beige dryness of the sand. Only voices of the wind. Cold nights with glittering stars your companions.

Great multitudes of people pressed upon your life to hear you and to be healed.

You are never more human to us than in those solitude seeking moments. Your energy spent in a ministry shadowed by recipients with challenging disbelief, dissension and discord.

You knew the wisdom of withdrawing into silence and solitude to pray.

We do not seek wilderness as You did. It comes upon us unawares. Our desert is concrete and cacophony. Air-conditioned. Cyber-space. Controlled access. MTV. Headline News.

Teach us the value, not the pain, of wilderness praying. Teach us how to follow Your example and seek Your will when our lives are dry and lonely. Remind us that we are never alone and without You in our wilderness. Teach us the ministry of wilderness praying.

Amen.

Morning Blessing

May you seek God early in your day and early in your struggle.

May you acknowledge your soul's thirst before the Divine Breakfast Companion who alone knows your inner desert.

May He meet you there in your own particular thirsty and dry land where hope eludes and trust diminishes.

May you remember having seen His power and His glory in the holy places of your life and heart.

May you drink the Living Water of Jesus Christ from His morning menu of grace and begin your day refreshed and filled with praise for Him.

Thanks be to God for His love.

Amen.

Psalm 63: 1-3

Wrestling Champ

May you have the determination to wrestle with God.

May you have the strength to not let him go until He blesses you with answers to your heart's deepest longings and questions.

May God bless you when he sees He cannot prevail against the strength of your prayers.

May the Peniel places of your broken-ness heal and be transformed by grace into wells of mercy for all who seek your guidance and companionship.

And may it be so for you now at this time of your need. This is my prayer for you from Gen. 32:26-31.

Amen.

Bereaved

Lord Jesus,

Look with care upon Your dear one who returns from the funeral, opens the front door, turns on the lights and is alone.

Except for you, Jesus.

Bless Your beloved bereaved through this difficult night and all the nights until reunited with the lost loved one in eternity.

Be present in the dinner hours, the special dates and anniversaries, the everyday tasks and trials, the ambush of emotion and exhaustion.

Comfort the tears with Your holy understanding as One who wept for Lazarus.

In the times of weeping, mercifully let a tear fall from Heaven to anoint this grieving heart with the Blessed Hope You are, Lord Jesus. Thank You.

    Amen.

    Jn. ll:33-35

Agent Orange

Jesus Christ is the same yesterday and today and forever.
Heb 13:8 (RSV)

Heavenly Father,

You created the universe and everything in it. Even Agent Orange. We come to You in prayer for one of Your children.

Mercifully reach down from Heaven to heal any past, present or future effects of Agent Orange in our friend's mind and body. Make this healing complete, last through his entire lifetime and bring him the immediate peace of Your Presence.

Bless with strength this fine husband, father, citizen and Viet Nam Veteran.

Even as he reads these words, help him know Your Son, Jesus Christ, in whose Name we pray, was with him in the jungles, is with him now at home and will be with him in eternity.

Thank You, Father.

Amen.

Grieving Heart

The Lord is near to the broken-hearted,
and saves the crushed in spirit.
Psalm 34:18 (NIV)

May He whose hands are nail-scarred hold your broken heart in His hands. May you feel His Presence, His touch, His love.

May all the fissures of pain in your heart be filled and comforted by the Holy Spirit.

May half of your heart, broken off from you in the death of your loved one, rest in eternity where there is no sickness, nor pain.

And may your remaining half-heart heal with joyful expectation of reunion. May it beat passionately, though fractured in half, for your Savior and for the life He has ahead for you until reunion. May this time given to you by God be a time of joy.

This is my prayer for you.

Amen.

A Zacchaeus Heart

May you know the joy of welcoming the Lord Jesus into your heart and home.

May your priorities and perspectives yield to preparations for the Divine Guest.

May you know He is sitting at the table, participating in the conversations, receiving the best recipe results of your life.

May the answering heart of Zacchaeus be yours in generous giving and restitution.

In hearing the blessed words, "Today salvation has come to this house," be strong in knowing He came to seek and to save you and your loved ones. For such a heart, I do pray for you.

Amen.

Luke 19:2-10 (RSV)

Bottle Deposit

Thou hast kept count of my tossings, Put thou my tears in Thy bottle!
Are they not in Thy book?
Psalm 56:8 (RSV)

Dear one who grieves,

Know the Lord God keeps count of your tossings, keeps count of the sleepless nights, the indecision, the confusion of feeling lost and alone.

Know that the Lord Jesus, who wept at the grave of Lazarus, wept beside you at the grave of your loved one.

Your tears are not a waste of despair, but a blessed accumulation in God's own heart.

When His heart bottle is full of your tears, He will dispense them in the form of grace to other bereft persons you encounter.

Be blessed by my prayer for you. Please likewise pray for me.

Let us together thank God for keeping our tears in His heart as a bottle deposit of comfort and grace in our grief.

Amen.

Adoption

My prayer for you is that by the revelation of the Holy Spirit, you will understand God planned to adopt you as His son through Jesus Christ.

He planned for you, prepared a crib and painted a nursery for you in his divine heart-home. He freely gave Jesus Christ to you that baptized into Christ, you would be a well-dressed child, clothed in Christ.

May you fulfill all God's longings for you. May you speak and sing and pray words of praise for His glorious grace. May your faith grow. May you reflect God's love to all persons you greet.

And may you respond with joy to God's purpose and pleasure in giving you His Beloved Son, the Lord Jesus Christ, in whose Name I pray for you.

Amen.

Eph. 1:5 (NIV)

Beautiful Feet

How beautiful on the mountains are the feet
of those who bring good news.
Is.52:7 (NIV).

Dear Sister in the Lord Jesus,

May you be blessed with the Holy Spirit pedicure of beautiful feet.

Whatever mountains of fear, grief, illness, disappointed dreams and unmet needs loom over your life, may you remember your feet are beautiful, colorful and strong as they climb heights of faithfulness.

May you proclaim peace to all you pass on the path.

May your message of the good-tidings of salvation in Jesus Christ direct your steps with those beautiful feet.

Whether you wear sandals or slides, slippers or sneakers, high heels or boots, your feet are beautiful. May you be bold to remind your friends and family and fellowship in Zion that "Your God reigns."

Be blessed by His pedicure and my prayer.

Amen.

Hezekiah Heart

May a merciful God grant to you a Hezekiah heart of 2 Kings 18:3-6.

May you hold fast to Him and never waiver in keeping His Commandments.

May you be refreshed by His Holy Spirit as you walk before God on every path of your life.

May your whole-hearted devotion to your Savior strengthen you to smash the altars of other gods and destroy their call to you.

May God's grace be upon all you undertake for success in His Name. As Isaiah extended the healing benediction of God to Hezekiah, so I to you:

> "This is what the Lord, the God of your father David says, 'I have heard your prayers and seen your tears; I will heal you. '"
> 2 Kings 20:5 (NIV) .

Be healed, dear one in the faith.
Amen.

An Abraham Blessing for You

... but Abraham still stood before the Lord. Gen 18 :22 (RSV).

May the Holy Spirit, the Spirit of Prayer, encourage you to pray. May you have the strength to still stand before the Lord in prayer.

May Abraham's bartering compassion direct your prayers to the heart of God. May your own heart have passion for God's lost ones, especially those in your own life.

Dear Friend in Faith, please pray for me that in all my struggles with sin and sorrow, I might still stand in prayer.

Amen.

Novena

Spirit of Prayer,

In Your mercy, hear my prayer for a dear woman whose name is known only to God, but not to me. I pray You will relieve the anguish of heart behind the words printed in a Saturday morning newspaper on the Feast of St. Jude.

Comfort and instruct her in the truth that the Lord Jesus Christ is sitting at the Father's right hand ever interceding for her and her loved ones. Transfer her devotion and intensity to Jesus Christ. But the most important bidding, Gentle Spirit, is that her faith be answered lest she despair.

Behind these words printed in a newspaper, there must be an alcoholic husband, a daughter with breast cancer, unpaid bills, varicosities from waitressing, a faithful one who receives the Bread come down from Heaven every Sunday.

Come, Holy Spirit, to her in the revelation of Jesus Christ, whose Sweet Spirit You are.

Amen.

Heb 7:25

Thirsty

Yes, Lord,

We of the parched tongue seek Your favor.

The heights of our prideful acquisition are bare; our valleys are low and lonely; our everyday is a wilderness of responsibilities and repetition. You alone are the answer to our aridity.

Quench our souls in Your river of mercy. Bathe our spirits in Your pools of grace.

Refresh and renew us in the Divine and eternal fountain of Living Water, Your Son, The Lord Jesus Christ in whose name we pray. Thank You, Lord.

Amen.

Is 41:17-18

Nard Blessing

Dear sister,

May you open the sealed flask of your heart and pour its contents on the feet of Jesus. Costly contents of sorrow and sickness, discouraged dreams and discouraging people, sins and shortcomings, desperation and devotion. Costly contents anointing His feet.

> May you hear His words"…she has done a beautiful thing to me"
> (Mark 14:6; RSV).

May you know that your "…house is filled with the fragrance of the perfume" (John 12:3; RSV). The aroma of loving Jesus fills your home, your relationships, your service, your prayers.

The fragrance of your devotion to Jesus permeates rooms, opens doors, freshens curtains, carpets and concerns, freshens your heart with joy.

May all who visit your home and your heart experience the fragrance of Jesus.

May you be blessed by the words of this prayer, and likewise pray for me.

Amen.

Spring Cleaning

The curtain of the temple was torn in two from top to bottom.
Mark 15:38(RSV)

Dear sister,

As you tend to windows and carpets, closets and winter clothing, pause to remember the condition of the Curtain. It is torn in two from top to bottom. No seamstress nor dry cleaner need restore it.

It separated the Holy Place from the Most Holy Place.

At this time of the year, at this time of cleaning your soul and your house, remember Christ's death has opened to you a new and living way through the curtain of His body. Once and for all, you may enter the Most Holy Place of eternal redemption by His own blood.

Set aside the dust cloth and the distraction of your life.

Kneel for a moment and gaze at your own window curtains.

Be confident that your eternal redemption does not need an annual spring cleaning. It is sealed in eternity.

Thanks be to God for His Son, Jesus.

Amen.

Listening

May the grace of God amplify your hearing.

May you hear with clarity whatsoever God wants you to hear about Himself and about yourself.

May holy hearing bring you to repent the sin in your life, sin separating you from God and from the people He has placed in your life.

May you hear God's will for you amidst the noise of the world around you and the static of self within you.

May a most generous Lord turn up the volume of His Heart's love message to you.

And may you be blessed with the little kid's ears of Samuel to listen.

Amen.

1 Sam 3:9

Garden Blessing

May the Lord of all growth and gardens and godliness look down with favor upon you.

May you realize you are a well-watered garden, watered in the Living Water of Jesus Christ.

May you experience His continual guidance and strength to be satisfied with desire for good things.

May the Living Water of Jesus be in you a spring that never fails, a spring of refreshment to you and a refuge for the spiritually thirsty who seek the Lord in you.

May you blossom in your faith, dear gardener for God.

This is my prayer for you.

    Amen.

    Isaiah 58: 11

The Blessing of Belief

Blessed is she who has believed that what the Lord
has said to her will be accomplished.
Luke 1:45(NIV)

Beautiful sister,

May blessed belief be your gift from God.

May blessed belief inform your decisions, steady your emotions, direct all your responses and relationships.

May blessed belief remind you that what the Lord has spoken to your heart and prompted you to pray will be accomplished.

May blessed belief tune your ear to hear His Word and His words to you.

May blessed belief guide you into undreamed dimensions of closeness and communication with the Lord Jesus, in Whose Name I pray for you.

May you be blessed by what the Lord has spoken to you and by my prayer for you.

Amen.

Heart Shards

Lord Jesus,

See all those heart shards?

They are fragments, broken off from a praying heart. Shards lifted up to You in prayer: pieces of praise and petition, moments of repentance and remembered failures, intercessions for loved ones and shadows of bereavement.

In Your great mercy, regard the heart shards of the dear one who reads this prayer. Gather the fragments into Your Divine Heart.

Respond by returning prayer pieces in the shape of blessings: strength of faith, hope of mind, health of body, direction in distress, joy in worship.

May every prayer, every heart shard of this dear one, be returned in blessing. Thank You, Jesus.

Amen.

Heb.13:9

Sacred Sweetness

How sweet is your love, my sister, my bride.
Songs 4:10(RSV)

Dear sister,

Your love is sweet to the Lord Jesus.

Your every thought, prayer, praise bring sweetness to His Divine Heart. As a child delights in candy, so your love delights your Savior. It is a holy sweetness in you no sugar substitute of worldly care can replicate.

You are the Dessert of the Divine, a confection of creation, covered with the icing of the Holy Spirit. Even your most desperate or distracted prayer is honey in Heaven.

You are His sister of His own speaking in Matthew 12:50.

You are His bride of Revelation 22:17.

May you remain sweet in Christ Jesus.

Sweet of soul to worship Him.

Sweet of spirit to hear Him.

Sweet of speech to praise Him.

Sweet of gesture and generosity to serve Him.

Sweet of faith to trust Him in your struggles and sorrows.

Sweet sister, be reminded of your unique sacred sweetness, and, likewise remind me.

Amen.

Bereavement Blessing

For you, O Lord, have delivered my soul from death,
my eyes from tears, my feet from stumbling,
Psalm 116:8(NIV)

May your soul return to its rest in the words of Psalm 116.

May the cords of grief encompassing your heart be loosened by a merciful God that you might now walk in the land of the living, walk with confidence into the life He has for you, walk, knowing He will keep your feet from stumbling in decisions, choices, relationships. He has loosed the cords of death and you can stride in His protective Presence.

May you know His love has delivered you from the death of courage in your bereavement.

May you be healed by the holy truth that your beloved's death was precious in the sight of the Lord who welcomes those who love Him into eternity. Precious also to the Lord is your remaining life.

May you continue to love the Lord because He has heard your voice and your supplications.

May you be blessed by the words of this prayer and likewise pray for me.

Amen.

Answering

May the Lord answer you when you are in distress,
May the name of the God of Jacob protect you.
Psalm 20:1(NIV)

Dear Sister,

May each day begin for you with the blessing of His Presence in your heart.

May you know the Lord Jesus hears you and answers your prayers.

May the everydayness of distress and dysfunction, problems and personalities, tensions and tiredness yield to His answering love for you.

May you be protected by the Holy Name of Jesus, surrounding you, shielding you, separating you from the darkness of the world.

May you remember my prayer for you and likewise pray for me, a sister struggler in the Kingdom of God.

Thanks be to God who answers prayers.

Amen

Green Card

Lord Jesus Christ,

All praise to You, our Constant Companion, in this temporary worker status on earth.

We are strangers here on a permit whose length of days is known only to You. Because we do not know when it will expire, our vision is blurred by people, problems and pressures of everydayness.

Migrants as we are, the temptations of a culture foreign to our God are ever before us, its language alien to our hearts.

Mercifully sustain us with Your grace in our sojourn towards eternity.

Mercifully transform our green card time into preparation for our true home, the city whose builder and maker is God.

Thank You, Lord Jesus Christ.

Amen.

Heb.ll:10-13

CANCER PATIENTS

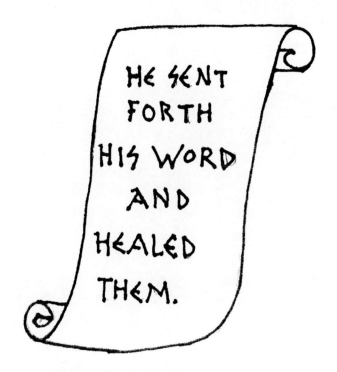

HE SENT
FORTH
HIS WORD
AND
HEALED
THEM.

PSALM 107:20

Homecoming

Behold, I stand at the door and knock.
Rev. 3:20 (RSV)

Lord Jesus,

How many doors You have stood beside and knocked.

In Your mercy, open the door of this home and go in. The occupant is not home yet, but en route from the hospital with a suitcase and a heavy heart.

Cancer diagnosis, Lord.

O, Lord, go now from room to room, filling it with Your love and Your Divine Presence, because cancer is such a lonely illness. Bring healing and strength here.

Bid Your Holy Spirit of Comfort to linger here that Your dear child with cancer might open the door of home and of heart to a renewed blossoming of hope.

Great Physician, thank You for this house call of healing.

Amen.

Diagnosis

The people who sat in darkness have seen a great light, and for those
who sat in the region and shadow of death light has dawned.
Matthew 4: 16 (RSV)

Beloved friend,

As you sit in hospital waiting rooms and doctors' offices, may the
great light of God's love illuminate your cancer diagnosis.

May the region of tests, treatments and therapies become a time of
seeing God's mercy in your heart, relationships and life.

May the incandescence of God's grace fill you with hope each dawn
of every day.

And may you know He who is no stranger to pain, scars and suffering
on the Cross, the Lord Jesus, reaches His healing hand to hold yours.

Amen.

House Call

So the sisters sent word to Jesus, "Lord the one You love is sick."
John 11:3(NIV)

Great Physician,

In Your mercy make a house call upon Your loved one and our loved one.

Place Your sacred stethoscope where it will hear the longings of his heart for Your peace. Take his wrist in Your nail-scarred hand to feel the pulse of desire for You. Dispense Your grace with generosity; it is the only enduring medication.

Write a prescription for forgiveness and hope. And do leave a Divine appointment card reminder for an office visit to You in eternity.

Thank You, Lord Jesus, for this *cita divina*.

Amen.

Morning Prayer

Let the morning bring me word of Your unfailing love,
for I have put my trust in You.
Show me the way I should go, for to You I lift up my soul.
Psalm 143:8 (NIV)

Lord Jesus, Bright Morning Star,

Illuminate with Your love the morning of this dear sister who awakens to another day of cancer.

Remind her anew of Your Holy Presence.

Send Your Light of Love into today's morning light that can only faintly dispel a day of medication, blood tests, radiation treatment and discouragement.

Mercifully show her the way she should go through the maze of medical decisions and protocols.

Be reminded she puts her trust in You. Be reminded of her sweetness of spirit. Dayspring. Light of the World. Incandescence of God, shine into her day.

Thank You, Lord Jesus.

Amen.

Fringe Benefits

For Melanie

Take courage, dear one who is ill.

The Lord Jesus has traveled through eternity to you. Recognize the Lord Jesus is there in the place you are in now.

He is close enough for you to reach out and touch. Remember His mercy and His miracles.

In the assurance of memory, reach out to Him for healing. Take my hand in these words of prayer.

Touch the fringe of His garment.

Receive His healing and His love for you.

Let us together give thanks unto God that you are well.

Amen.

Matt. 14:35-36(RSV)

Chemotherapy Prayer

... a bruised reed he will not break,
and a dimly burning wick he will not quench.
Isaiah 42:3 (RSV)

O, Lord,

Hear this prayer for a dear one undergoing chemotherapy treatments. The bruises, Lord. On arms and hands, even on feet from seeking a sturdy vein. Purple. Painful. Depersonalizing.

You tell us You will not break a bruised reed. Send sufficient grace to steady the spirit of a bruised reed in chemotherapy.

You see, Lord, courage and faith smolder and sputter in the heart of Your beloved child struggling with cancer.

In Your mercy, fan this dimly burning faith into bright strength of heart and of hope in You, Jesus, our Blessed Hope.

Amen.

Chemotherapy Prayer 2

I am poured out like water, and all my bones are out of joint, my
heart is like wax, it is melted within my breast.
Psalm 22: 14 (RSV)

Lord God,

In Your mercy, hear this prayer for our friend and brother undergoing
chemotherapy.

How apt Your Scripture to one whose life seems poured out like
water; out of control. Flowing away. Bones aching and out of joint;
courage melting as wax in a candle; blood counts and bruises; needles
and nausea.

Reach down from Heaven to touch this dear one with Your own
nail-scarred hands that he might know he is not in the dust to die, but
in the hands of Your love.

Be his strength when his own strength is all dried up, for he has
great love of you.

How we will praise You among the people, for You have not hidden
Your face from the suffering of the afflicted. Thank You, Lord.

Amen.

Chemotherapy Prayer 3

O taste and see that the Lord is good!
Happy is the man who takes refuge in Him.
Psalm 34:8 (RSV)

Merciful Savior,

Through the mystery of your grace, give to this dear one spiritual taste buds surpassing those effected by chemotherapy. Grant such a taste of You, Jesus, the Bread come down form Heaven, that Your suffering child might see You in each event and experience of this cancer.

Be generous in the grace of heavenly happiness to trust in You during those moments when treatments overwhelm and courage deserts. Send Your Holy Angels to encamp around and to protect with Your love Your own beloved child in chemo. Thank You, Lord.

Amen.

Nighttime Prayer

My soul yearns for You in the night,
My spirit within me earnestly seeks thee.
Is. 26:9(RSV)

Lord God,

The night is such a rough time

When the house is quiet and dark and my spouse is sleeping the needed rest of a devoted caregiver, my pain seems worse. At such times, there are not distractions and activities to keep my mind occupied with thoughts other than cancer. If I take more medication, the burning edge of pain smolders but is not extinguished. Time becomes distorted; dreams disturb me; my emotions churn, fear visits me.

O God, my spirit seeks Thee.

Come to me, Spirit of the Living God, at night.

Come into my heart.

Come into my pain.

Come into my cancer that I might know Your healing grace. By a miracle of Your healing Power, change the darkness of my nights into the Light of Jesus Christ, Your Son, in whose Name I pray.

Thank You, God.

Amen.

Nighttime Visitor

I bless the Lord who gives me counsel; in the night also my heart instructs me. I keep the Lord always before me; because he is at my right hand, I shall not be moved.
Psalm 16:7-8 (RSV)

O God,

How difficult is the night for one who is not well.

The darkness. The isolation. And, yes, the physical pain. The memories.

Be merciful to Your dear servant who is ill. Instruct his heart during the nights. Instruct him in special and personal ways that You love him; You understand him; You are present with him. He has thus instructed many of us in Your church.

Be good to this dear brother and friend, for I pray in the Name of Your Son Jesus Christ who spent some difficult nights Himself.

Thank You, O God, for Your faithfulness to all who cry out to You.

Amen.

Hospital Visit of Jesus

Precious in the sight of the Lord is the death of his saints.
Psalm 116:15 (RSV)

Go, Lord,

Go quickly and quietly to this dear one who is dying in the hospital. Sit there on the bed beside her; comfort her, assure her of Your great love for her; show her Your own scars.

You are no stranger to her physical pain; You experienced Your own pain on The Cross.

Strengthen her with a glimpse of the Heavenly Jerusalem awaiting her after the long struggle with cancer. Make it possible for her to communicate that glimpse of peace with her family that they might come into stronger peace and faith.

In Your mercy, hear my prayer and go.

Amen.

Memorial Prayer

Almighty God,

We thank You for the life of Violet, Your precious daughter, who blossomed late in her life into the Kingdom of God.

We thank You that the suffering of cancer could be transformed for her into an opportunity to know Your love. And we thank You for the Resurrection of Your Son, Jesus Christ, because it assures us all the pain and tears are gone from those violet blue eyes in her new life in You.

Bless now her dear ones who grieve.

Bless the faithful congregants of this church who welcomed her into their hearts and their parish as a prelude to Your welcome of Violet into eternal life.

In the Name of Your Son, Jesus Christ, we pray.

Amen.

Rev. 21:4

Memorial

A woman unto women,
Nourishing, teaching, encouraging,
Modeling love of Redeemer,
Of husband, child, home, church.
Silhouette of strength, we stretched
In growth to your outline in cancer.

You waited for the light.
Outside the hospital window
Fathoms of indigo yielded
Ripples of mauve then pink.
Before we could say goodbye,
You traded the light for the Light.

Paradigm of pain with grace,
Your presence left us strong.
Reaching out now to others,
We see your silhouette in the Cross,
Your light now radiant in the Light,
Refracted to us by the heart of God.

For Discovery Weekend (1982)

Heavenly Father,

We praise You and thank You for Your steadfast love that endures forever.

We acknowledge You as the Author of all creation and the source of all blessings.

In particular, we ask You to bless the Discovery Weekend program with Your guidance and wisdom. We beseech You to release funds to the Discovery Weekend Foundation that our work may continue for Your children who suffer from cancer.

Many of them sit in the darkness of suffering and are in the shadow of death.

Father, we would share the Dayspring, the Lord Jesus Christ, with these cancer patients and their families. In Your mercy, establish and prosper our work. And guide our feet into the way of peace. Thank You, Lord.

      Amen.

      Luke 1:79

Discovery Weekend, 1985

Lord God,

We praise You and we thank You for Your love for us, for sending to us the Light of Jesus Christ, Your only-begotten Son.

We thank You for gathering us here together on this weekend that we might discover more of You in us and in our struggle with cancer.

Bless us each as we go our way, whatever the destinations, the decisions and the directions our journey with cancer will require of us.

We would be valiant travelers and can but ask Your strength to accompany us and ease the terrain ahead.

In Your holy generosity, give us grace in facing our future with faith in You and with prayer for one another.

These requests we make in the Name of Your Son, our Savior, Jesus Christ.

Amen.

John 1:4-5

For American Cancer Society
Sabbath 13 April 1986

... then from my flesh I shall see God, whom I shall see on my side,
and my eyes shall behold, and not as a stranger.
Job 19:26-27 (RSV)

Lord Jesus Christ,

In Your mercy, reveal Yourself to Your precious children who suffer with cancer.

Because You are no stranger to pain and suffering on the Cross, comfort cancer patients with a message of Your love for them.

Heal them; send Your Holy Spirit to strengthen them; deliver them from despair.

We pray Your reconciliation into the Kingdom of God would go forth from this prayer to the hearts of cancer patients. Whatever the course of their disease or the condition of their souls, may all come into such faith that they might stand in eternity in Your Presence and see You not as a stranger.

We beseech Your mercy and praise Your glory, In the Name of the Father, Son and Holy Spirit.

Amen.

Mary's Walk

Almighty God,

Thank You for the success of Mary's Walk.

Bless the Libby family, from the youngest to the oldest, for their planning and providing Mary's Walk. Fill their hearts with gratitude for Your Holy Presence in honoring Mary's memory.

Bless each staff member, volunteer and participant with the unique happiness only You create. From the first brochure mailed to the last walker or runner to finish, let Your hand of grace be upon all who entered into this great effort of mercy.

Bless each and every dollar donated to Mary's Walk. Place Your healing hand upon the research efforts that Your children who suffer from cancer might be helped by Your blessing upon Mary's Walk. Hear this prayer in the Name of Your Son, Jesus, the Physician and Healer of us all. Thank You, Lord.

Amen.

Voyage

Almighty God,

Bless each of our friends who sailed with us on the USS Discovery Weekend, for the seas of cancer are rough, and the voyage requires great courage.

In Your mercy, heal their bodies, calm their minds and hearts, strengthen their souls.

In the present storms and the future uncertainties, hold each one close to Your divine heart of love. Be to us all a compass of mercy, for there is none but You to guide us through the uncharted waters of a cancer diagnosis. Keep us ever aware of the sure and steadfast anchor of our souls, Your Son, Jesus Christ, in whose name we pray each day for our fellow crew members.

Amen.

Is 43:2

Anchor Prayer

We have this as a sure and steadfast anchor of the soul, a hope that enters into the inner shrine behind the curtain, where Jesus has gone as a forerunner on our behalf..
Heb 6: 19 (RSV)

Lord Jesus,

In Your mercy, hold fast this dear friend who sails the rough sea of cancer. High waves of treatments, medications, tests; harsh winds of pain and discouragement, dark skies of uncertainty about the future. Hold this precious sailor close to Your Divine Heart of Love that on the roughest days, Your Presence might be a sure and steadfast anchor of hope.

In You alone, Blessed Anchor, is strength and certainty.

Thank You, Lord.

Amen.

Discovery Weekend Dinner Grace

Lord God,

We pause a moment this evening to thank You for the many blessings, some of them perhaps even disguised as adversity, which You have given us today.

We thank You for the chance tonite to meet new friends and enjoy old ones.

Bless these gifts of food to the nourishment of our bodies, and as we share them together, incline our hearts to see in our midst, the opportunity to serve one another and to serve You, our Holy and Eternal God.

Amen.

(JHH 1991)

Discovery Weekend

"The Lord your God is in the midst of you."
Zephaniah 3:17 (RSV)

Heavenly Father,

How we thank You for our dear friends who experienced Discovery Weekend with us.

In Your mercy, heal the cancer which has overtaken their lives.

Let them know You are in the midst of every cell of their bodies, every treatment, every decision, every moment of their journey with cancer. Bless their loved ones who care and watch and wait.

Strengthen their hearts with a message of Your love and refresh them all with the healing presence of the Great Physician, Your Son, Jesus Christ, in whose Name we pray.

Amen.

POEMS

I WILL PRAISE GOD'S NAME IN SONG. AND GLORIFY HIM WITH THANKS~ GIVING.

PSALM 69:30

Sorrow

We travel together, Jesus and I, in a boat named Sorrow,
Sailing from curious crowds to a lonely place apart.
Memories our ballast, shifting and heavy, as we voyage.
Winds harsh, waves heaving, wide sky bereft of hope.
His cousin John leaped in utero recognition of Divinity,
My son John leaped in utero recognition of humanity.
Our grief's shore an uncharted place of shoals and rocks,
As He steadies the lines and watches the eternal horizon.
We seek a mooring where His pain speaks to mine,
Lest the frayed sheet of my faith be shredded and fail.
Gently He drops the anchor of my prayers over Sorrow's side,
To hold me by grace against the drifting of despair.
My compass the companionship of One winds and waves obey,
His Cross the mainmast reaching into an opening dawn.

   Now when Jesus heard this, He withdrew from there in a boat to a
lonely place apart.
      Mt. 14:13(RSV)

Love

Love is a holder of hands,
    a wiper of tears,
    a changer of diapers,
    a giver of blessing.

Love is a yielder of parking spaces,
    a holder of open doors,
    a wrapper of wedding gifts,
    a singer of Psalms.

Love is a finder of lost items,
    a cooker of pasta,
    a washer of lettuce,
    a reader of the Word.

Love is an emptier of trash,
    a folder of laundry,
    a laugher at self, not others,
    a kneeler in prayer.

Love is a sitter beside sickbeds,
    a forgetter of offense,
    a holder of tongue retort,
    a forgiver before being asked.

Love is a helper of the elderly,
    a soother of bruises ,
    a washer and ironer of shirts ,
    a burier of the dead.

Love is The Cross, two wood pieces
    looming over daily tasks,
    a nail-scarred hand reaching to
    grasp the holder of hands.

The Door

The porch whereon I expectantly stood,
Weighted with works I considered good,
Generosity, kindness, cards of support,
Surely could hold me in good report.
Efforts stored on my spiritual shelf,
Had amply provided calories of self.
The entry door remained a narrow fit,
No space to wedge myself through it.
Could effort and theology make me thin
With meetings and programs to begin?
Gym temples and diets fat-free and lite,
Cultural condiments denying the Light?
The Door opens only on a humble fast,
For entering where the first will be last.

Luke 13:22-30

Trees

In the shopping malls, restaurants, along streets and in offices,
on MTV, in parking lots,
I see men and women looking like trees walking.
Bodies groomed dieted, exercised, pierced, pedicured,
vitamined, telephoned, TV -ed,
Wooden hearts covered in the chic camo of casual.
Stands of maple, oak and elm close together in the darkness of
Trivia Forest. Touch my eyes again, Jesus, to clearly see
Your children of creation,
Where once I saw wooden men and women looking like trees walking.
Show me how the green-ness of grace opens leaves and limbs to the Light.
Speak words through me that wooden roots might thirst for the Living Water
of evergreen.

Mark 8:22-26

Poems

To Tom McKean
the other father in Heaven,

Hey, McKean are you listening up there?
Are you pulling with celestial prayer?

Our dear Molleye has come upon adversity,
An unexpected diagnosis of the Big C.

A lump appeared in her lovely right breast,
Now a medical maze, but you know the rest.

Put in a strong healing pitch, whatever you do,
To the Heavenly Father, who can pull her through.

Help us to bear the heavy prayer load,
For locating that one sentinel node.

You would be proud to see her, for sure,
Brave on the stretcher, calm and mature.

Preamble to uncertainly begins today,
What is ahead for her, only God can say.

While you play golf with the Heavenly Host,
Your prayers as her dad we value the most.

Ask for angels to bring healing energy
To Dr. Mills' hands for this lumpectomy.

Ask for strength and peace for our Molleye and then,
Add a dad's love and blessing to be our Amen.

The Plate

The plate slipped and shattered, or was it pushed
Into fragments of random flight across the floor?
Jagged jigsaw pieces now replaced the pictures
Once painted on the smooth surface of experience.
Marriage. Births. Deaths. Heartaches. Awakenings.
Memories. Sins. Defeats. Reconciliations. Prayers.
Then like a mother bending over a child in pain,
Not hesitating, questioning, using reason or logic,
He bent down from heaven to begin carefully
Collecting shards in His nail-scarred hands,
Reassembling them in the original heart shape,
Gluing them together with the mucilage of His love,
Replacing the mended plate on the working counter,
The cracked places stronger for touching His heart.

Is 61:1

Highway to Zion

In my spirit's travel, the odometer malfunctioned,
Causing me to surge ahead beyond the speed limit,
Passing slower hearts and in turn being passed.

Oncoming hearts with high beams blinding me
Into almost missing the sign for Baca Valley Exit,
Turning on to a barren terrain I never imagined.

Dry and flat and brown with no sign of rain,
Until The One who turned the water into wine
Brought unexpected pools to make barren Baca
A place of springs replenishing and strengthening,
For seeing the God of all of the gods in my life.

Psalm 84:5-7

Season

God, look down from Heaven above,
Bless two children in a season of love.
These dancers poised in love's cadence,
A pairing polarity, graced by innocence.
As summer light filters green and gold
On limbs and eyelids, angles and fold,
Let them burn to ash love's pure desire
Freeing a phoenix into the holiest fire.
When love's season becomes overgrown,
You part the play, but the friendship hone.
A season does a temporary growth imply,
An eternal harvesting follows for goodbye.
Until then, bless with forever their love to be
Holy in remembrance and sanctified by Thee.

Lazarus Lesson

"Lift the stone!"

Energy filled the tomb as His voice splintered darkness
Scraping reluctance as soul's stone cover begins to move
And Light filters onto bound hands and feet, limbs and life.

"Come forth!"

Had He also wept for my awakening from sin's slumber?
The voice a summons not a suggestion to respond and rise,
To move towards the opening where He waits as Light.

"Unwrap her!"

Helpful hands and hearts ease the painful peeling,
Removing tight transparent Saranwrap-sins of self
 His voice now kind, lifting me from my knees.

"Let her go home!"

Home to troubling tasks of being and becoming in Him
Penultimate homecoming preparing for another welcome
Into eternity where He waits for me with the porch light on.

John 11:38-44

Safekeeping

Lord,

Should You call me home today,
Watch over my loved ones, I do pray.
Keep Chris safe and alert as he flies,
Send angels to guard the Southwest skies.
Give Elise wisdom and faith to assure,
How deeply grateful I remain for her.
Young Joshua, who is a grandmom's joy,
Keep him healthy and careful as a boy.
To Charlotte grant fulfillment to see,
Her place is precious in our family.
Guide Paul in choices of church and career,
Remind him You are always standing near.
John, whose path has been alone and apart,
Has always been a joy to his mother's heart.
The gift of confidence, please for Melanie,
For a long productive life, being cancer free.
Forty-one years with my dearest Rabbit Jake
Staying in love with him for both our sakes.
Thank you for Jake and for being his wife,
It has been the better part of my earthly life,
In my leaving them, may Your lesson be,
How felicitous is the classroom of eternity.

1999

Drought

The ice cube tray empty, faucets ran dry,
No promise of rain in a flat and hot sky.
Dry soap and laundry filled the washing machine,
Shower head sputtered, kettle no whistling steam.
Lonely footsteps on my soul's desert sand,
No friend present to even hold my hand.
Courage gone, all energy replaced by fear,
Eyes void of vision and without a tear.
If a parched throat could scarcely pray,
Is the Scripture cistern empty that day?
Drought shapes a habit forgetting to see,
Grace replies, "All my springs are in Thee."

Psalm 87:7 (RSV)

The Red Hat

"Here. Take this hat. You look cold."
Cold she was, in a wheelchair, gray blanket, 14 degree temp.
Faded green snow parka, surgical stockings,
No shoes on feet propped on foot rests.
Her hair dirty blonde strings, roots black.
But young. Too young to sit in a wheelchair at the hospital entrance
Waiting for a taxi to take her home to a second floor apartment
        above Congress Street.
Too young for cocaine and beer, candles and contraception.
Too young for pain.
A mastectomy? Miscarriage? Midnight drunken battering?
The man behind her seedy, older, puffing on a cigarette worth
        leaving the warmth of the hospital lobby.
Startled, she looked up at me with the hard and flat glance of poverty.
Without a word, it said, "What do you want from me, you in a
        navy winter coat like that?"
"What can I pay you for it?" she asked as she covered the blonde
        strings with my hat.
"Nothing," I answered embarrassed.
Turning to enter the hospital, a second thought. "Pray for me.
I've been there myself, where you are.
        And I will pray for you."
"O.K, lady with the red hat, I will. Thanks."

Ecstasy

The ecstasy you are to me
Signals of a holy courtesy.
Introduction to be a part
Of eternity in God's heart.
A heaven of now being there,
Is consummated with a prayer,
Among saints who sing and pray,
As angels fold their wings away.

The Cage

A cage I built carefully through the years
Iron bars of memories, anxieties and fears.
Tight and secret, secured with a lock of self,
I placed my cage high on my soul's top shelf.
Interactions, abrasions, frustrations, and then
Ego would speak to take the cage down again,
To peer between its bars, revisit and see
Past hurts, neglects, unkindness to me.
Until a strange visitor my cage did embrace,
Divine Guest, called by the name of grace.
The lock vanished and the bars opened wide,
Unforgiven residents then tumbled outside.
Alone in my cage, whatever would I do?
He replied, "Behold, I make all things new.
Your cage now empty, your own past set free,
Celebrate the present, dance the future with Me."

Cell Phones

In airports, gas stations, dentists' waiting rooms, parking lots,
   shopping malls, elevators, fast food lanes, department store aisles,
   pharmacy check out lines, lavatory stalls, mammogram facilities,

At bus stops, train stations, magazine racks, traffic left turn lanes, auto
   repair shops, restaurant tables, soft ice cream cone windows,

On park benches, escalators, jogging paths, beaches, wilderness hiking
   trails, bicycles, treadmills, buses,

In SUVs, Hondas, pick-ups, Fords,

Voices. Words. The personal made public. The babble of the banal.
   Sacred sensibility shared in the auditorium of hurry.

Amplification of anxiety.
   Questions. Comments. Chatter. Commands. Requests. Criticisms.
      Teenage voices planning parties.
      Middle-age voices directing domesticity.
      Executive voices giving orders.
      Female voices gossiping.
      Male voices Monday quarterbacking.

Unable to hear The Word made flesh.

Emptiness echoing into eternity where The Living Word waits to be
   heard.

Mt. 11:15

Spring Growth

It will be forever spring,
Tree buds yearning to open,
Nacre nimbus of fog on roofs,
Finches half dressed in gold,
Erect crocus amid dead leaves.

The yellow surprise of forsythia,
An earth moist and welcoming.
Heart sheds its winter silhouette
To emerge as wonder and change.

The Resurrection. And loving you.

Volunteer

The child was without defense, no helper could be found,
Submerged by environment, dark, unhealthy and unsound.
For bad behaviors, sins, stumblings into wrong choice,
For disobedience and rebellion, the child had no voice.
A full investigation was ordered by the Appellate Court
The Judge appointed Volunteer to present a final report.
The Volunteer attorney prepared a miraculous brief
Against Satan's tribunal of punishment and no relief.
Into the courtroom the Volunteer carried a strange tree,
Its evidence shaped as a Cross would set the child free,
The Judge of Superior Court deliberated on His decree,
And reversed the lower tribunal, the child was not guilty.
Jesus, our Guardian Ad Litem, hear our prayer and plea,
Defend all Your children on the court docket of eternity.

1 John 2:1

Closets

The closets needed cleaning, spring was drawing near
Shelves, crannies and nooks of items once held dear.
Blouses without buttons, no zippers on skirts,
Jeans no longer fit and big-shouldered shirts.
Unmatched stockings, shoes with heels too high,
Colors, shapes, styles in fashions since gone by.
One dark and cluttered area seldom ever seen,
A different heart storage, needing to be clean.
Unhemmed forgiveness and unzipped dreams,
Neglects and resentments ripped out at the seams.
Gossip, criticism, quarrels and those secret fears,
Kept my heart a cluttered closet all these years.
Hurts, ambitions, angers never put to rest,
Faded attitudes hidden by my Sunday best.
Shoes worn on paths they should not have gone,
Gestures of kindness and mercy never tried on.
Discordant jangling hangers over an empty bin,
A careful closet cleaning to rid my heart of sin.
The wardrobe I needed is different in cut and design,
Fabric never fades or tears a style uniquely mine.
The Divine Tailor creates the outfits for my station,
His grace clothes me with garments of salvation.

Is.61:10

HOLIDAYS

SEASONS
OF JOY
AND
GLADNESS
AND
CHEERFUL
FEASTS.

ZECHARIAH 8:19

Advent Prayer

Blessed are the people who know the festal shout,
who walk, 0 Lord, in the light of Your countenance.
Psalm 89:15 (RSV)

May you walk in His light this Advent.

May you awaken each morning with welcome for the light of day and for the Light of Christ in your life.

May the true Light, Jesus Christ, whose coming into the world we celebrate at Christmas, light your personal journey to Bethlehem.

May you wear the armor of Light as you travel towards Him. This is my prayer for you, dear one in the faith.

Amen.

Advent

Blessed Lord Jesus, Holy One who approaches during Advent that our hearts might be prepared to see You at Your appearing,

Mercifully grant to us the strength to renounce worldly passions and pursuits of the Christmas season, surrounded as we are by celebration not of You.

Mercifully bestow upon us the wisdom to prepare for the holiday reminder of Your Incarnation.

Mercifully enable us to articulate to our contemporaries, the blessed hope You are, Lord Jesus.

We await Your appearing in the Christ Child of Christmas and in the glory of our great God and Savior.

Amen.

Titus 2:11-14

John Home for Christmas

On that day I will gather you together and bring you home again.
Zeph. 3:20 (NLT)

The angels have hung up your stockings, and all of creation has decorated your Christmas tree with celestial galaxies bright beyond imagining. Saints with spirits made perfect have helped wrap gifts and placed them under your first Home for Christmas tree.

You will open the gifts slowly and meditatively, as you always did here on earth. A big red bow is tied around peace. Your troubled young mind can now be at peace. You understand how truly you were loved by God and by us.

Another gift box contains the healing and restoration of all your relationships. Whatever was left unresolved here is restored in eternity, because God's time is without limit.

The Christmas music you began enjoying at Halloween is beautiful and harmonious, because God is the Master Caroler.

You are home now in the will of God.

You were created in the heart of God.

And He welcomes your return.

You are home for Christmas.

Christmas Preparations

"In the wilderness prepare the way of the Lord,
Make straight in the desert a highway for our God.
Isaiah 40:3 (RSV).

Whatever the desert of your heart this Christmas, may the grace of God prepare in you a highway to our God.

May you travel on His Holy Highway to Bethlehem where the miracle of Christ's birth will heal you.

May your journey strengthen you to encourage a highway to our God in the lives and in the hearts of the wilderness dwellers in your life.

A Blessed Christmas to you, dear wilderness sojourner in the faith.

Amen.

Christmas Light

The true light that enlightens everyman was coming into the world.
John 1:9 (RSV)

Lord Jesus Christ, True Light,

In the darkness of winter and the darkness of our lives, illuminate Christmas with Your Holy Presence.

Illuminate our hearts with expectation.

Illuminate our choices, activities and expenditures with wisdom.

Illuminate our relationships with love that we might abide in the Light.

Illuminate with grace our homes, bright as they are with Christmas tree lights, candles and porch decorations.

We fling wide the cupboards and closets of our Christmas hearts, asking You to shine into every shelf and corner of sin and self.

How dark our world; how bright our Christ. Come to us, Light of the World.

Incandescence of God, Christmas Light. Come to us.

Amen.

A Christmas Prayer for You

We pray for you and for God's blessings to be with you this Christmas of 1990.

May your heart travel to the city of David to welcome a Savior who is Christ the Lord.

May you hear the angels' song and recognize Him as described by the angels ... a great joy.

In His presence this Christmas, may you experience a fullness of joy.

May His joy be in your heart and your home, present at your table, and illuminate your celebration.

Please remember with us in prayer our dear friends, the cancer patients and their loved ones, that they might travel to the Savior who will carry their burdens.

May you realize by our greeting that it is a privilege for us to journey with you towards the Savior of us all.

Amen.

Luke 2:10

When the angels went up from them into heaven, the shepherds said
to one another, "Let us go over to Bethlehem to see this thing that
has happened which the Lord has made known to us."
Luke 2:15(RSV)

Let us go to Bethlehem this Christmas of 2004.

Let us go again to see in our hearts the miracle of the Word made
flesh which the Lord has made known to us.

Let us go from the frenzy of the season, the plastic decorations and
smiles, the pressure of preparations, the nostalgia for the lost ones.

Let us go from terrorism, war in Iraq, air pollution, AIDS, auto
accidents, corporate theft, political rant, spy satellites, cultic religions,
commerce and materialism.

Let us go to Bethlehem in the company of all the saints who have
made this holy pilgrimage of the heart.

Let us travel in encouragement and in prayer for the cancer patients
and their loved ones that they might experience healing and comfort
in the love of God.

Let us go to Bethlehem where we receive the Savior God has sent
to us.

Then strengthened in our wills by the grace of God, let us, like the
shepherds and the Wise men, return glorifying and praising God.

Amen.

Christmas Grief

May you be comforted by a glimpse of God's love for you this Christmas.

May your broken heart be bandaged by the nail-scarred hands of Jesus. May He give you the oil of gladness instead of mourning.

May every Christmas tree, sprig of holly, green wreath you see become a garland of praise instead of ashes in your heart.

May God's mercy change your faint spirit into a mantle of praise.

May you dress your heart with the mantle of praise every day of the holiday season, because your loved one is with Him.

Accept my prayer for you, beloved friend, who grieves this Christmas.

Amen.

Isaiah 61:3

Christmas Cancer

For God so loved the world that He gave His only Son, that whoever believes in Him should not perish but have eternal life.
John 3:16 (RSV)

Almighty God,

We pray for our dear friends who have cancer and for their loved ones this Christmas. Each one who receives our greeting is a special blessing to us. They are precious to us as they are to You. We lift them to You for the miracle and the mercy of healing in body, mind and spirit.

Through the working of Your Holy Spirit, be for them an astonishment of joy in Your Gift of Jesus Christ, the One who came into a world of problems and pain and illness that we might know Your love. May their hearts travel to Bethlehem on a special journey of peace and hope. Hear our prayer for each one who receives our greeting, for we pray in the Name of Your Son, Jesus Christ.

Amen.

Christmas Companion

... and they will call him Immanuel-which means, "God with us".
Matthew 1:23 (NIV)

My prayer for you is that you might experience Immanuel-God - with-you, this Christmas.

May Immanuel-God-with-you, grant you excellence in your work, safety in your travel, and holy hospitality in your home.

May Immanuel-God-with-you, grant the desires of your heart and answer your prayers.

May Immanuel-God-with-you, reveal His perfect will to you and grant you the strength of follow it.

May Immanuel-God-with-you, bless and heal our beloved friends who have cancer and sustain their loved ones.

May Immanuel-God-with-you, greet your soul's pilgrimage to Bethlehem with His gift of joy.

May Immanuel-God-with-you, the Lord Jesus Christ, bless each day of the New Year in your life. He has certainly blessed us with you.

Amen.

Creator as Caroler

The Lord your God is in your midst, a warrior who gives victory; He
will rejoice over you with gladness
He will renew you in His love;
He will exult over you with loud singing.
Zeph. 3: 17 (RSV)

Hear the melody of His song above the music of Christmas:

All you stars and planets and celestial creations; sun, moon, galaxies
and meteors, hear the strains of song.

All you rains and snows and winds and sunspots, hear His singing.

All you angels in Heaven or on assignment, fold your wings to
listen.

All you restless oceans and rocky shores, all you continents, streams,
rivers and mountains, cease your activity to hear.

All you saints on earth, His people who turn to Him in their hearts,
pause to hear God's voice in song.

He who created all things on earth and in heaven, the Creator God
who was before all time and in all time, is singing over us.

The Creator Caroler, the God of all that exists and will exist, is
rejoicing in song and renewing us in His love.

Hear His song and know you are loved by the Creator Caroler and
by me this Christmas.

Holiday Prayer for Chris

Almighty God,

In Your great mercy, alert Your holy angels to heightened protection of Chris during the holidays. As the national Day of Thanksgiving and the holy time of Christmas approach, the increase in air travel brings an increase in safety and security concerns.

Whether in a big airport terminal or a small SWA station, keep him safe in his plane, safe on the ramps and runways and gates, safe in hotels and safe in travel to and from his flights, safe in the skies of Your creation.

Be generous in grace to Chris that his heart might be at peace in the assurance of Your love and protection for him during the holidays.

We ask this blessing upon Chris in the Name Your Son, Jesus Christ, whose own redeemed Chris is. Thank You, Father.

Amen.

Psalm 91

Root Cellar Christmas Eve

Almighty God,

May all who enter the Root Cellar on this Christmas Eve 2004, be touched by your Holy Spirit.

May the journey to 94 Washington Street, whatever its purpose, be spiritually symbolic of the heart's journey to Bethlehem.

May awakened faith and renewed encouragement be the Root Cellar's gift to all who enter its doors.

In particular, hear this prayer for the food distribution day that every soul present be saved.

May none take home produce, meat and bread, without also taking home the Bread of Life, Jesus Christ, Your Son, in whose Name we pray.

Thank You, Father.

Amen.

John 6:35

Bethlehem Intersection

Take no gold, nor silver, nor copper in your belts,
no bag for your journey...
Matt.10:10(RSV)

Jesus, Journeying One,
   Your Nativity approaches.
   You travel through history towards our celebration of Your birth.
   You travel from eternity towards our Christmas.
   You travel through our sins and errors, weakness of will. You travel through our experiences, around our baggage of foolish vain desires and inappropriate attempts at religion to better know You.
   We travel to You, to Bethlehem of the Heart, through the crush and press of the holiday expectations.
   We travel to You through time pressures to perform, to render happiness of Christmas to our loved ones via plastic presentations and pumped up praise.
   Our junction is the Bethlehem Intersection where Your eternal glory and generosity meet our ephemeral existence. In Your mercy, prevent us from taking a wrong turn, for pulling off the heart highway to You, for parking distractions and soul tanks on empty.
   Bring us safely to the Christmas fullness of the Bethlehem Intersection.
      Amen

A New Year Prayer for You

May the God of Hope reside in your heart each day of the New Year. May it be for you a year of joy in His salvation of your soul; joy in His message of love to you in Scripture; joy in His strength available to you in the Holy Spirit. May it be for you a year of peace in your family and personal relationships; peace in your tasks and travel; peace in your soul.

May the Holy Spirit fill you anew with such power that You will overflow with hope for yourself, for your loved ones and for your church. May all persons you meet experience the Christ within you.

And may He who is the Alpha and the Omega, the First and the Last, our Blessed Hope Jesus, make all things new for you in the New Year. May Jesus Christ be with you on the first as on the last day of the New Year.

Amen.

Rev 21:5

Happy Valentine's Day

We wanted you to celebrate this day of hearts, love and cupids.

The best Valentine is God's love. He has a weird and wonderful way of loving you just as you are, regardless of what has happened in your life.

Jesus believes you are special, important and unique. A long time ago, He was a boy exactly the age you are now. He also did jail time. He understands where you are. He wants to be your friend. Why not give Him a try?

Easter

He is not here; for he has risen, as he said.
Matthew 28:6 (RSV)

Risen Christ,

All Praise and glory are Yours.

You have been victorious over sin and death that we might be forgiven our sins and have eternal life with You and the Father of Heaven.

In Your Risen Glory, reach down to us as we struggle with the darkness of our own spiritual tombs. In Your mercy, free us from dead works, dead faith and dead intentions. Strengthen us to understand that if we are to be glorified with You, we must also suffer with You through this Passion Week. Reveal Yourself to us on Easter morning; renew our hearts and our lives to proclaim Your Resurrection.

Grant these blessings upon each dear one who receives our Easter greeting. Be glorified in us all, Lord Jesus Christ.

Amen.

Easter

May the Risen Christ bless you this Easter.

May you experience anew His power each time you exchange the greeting, "He is Risen!"

May His Holy Spirit rekindle your awe at the Resurrection.

May your home be a haven of peace and your loved ones add their joy to yours.

May the Risen Lord Jesus Christ Himself appear in your heart and show you His nail-scarred hands and feet are your healing.

May the Lord Jesus, who prays for you at the right hand of God, hear my prayers for you and add them to His own.

Happy Easter, dear one in the faith.

Amen.

Easter in a Nursing Home

Dear Friend in the Lord,

Are there stones rolled over your heart, as was a stone over the tomb of Jesus?

Stones of grief for your loved ones lost to death.

Stones of illness and physical pain, medication and doctor's appointments.

Stones of confinement to a wheel chair, a walker, a semi-private small space of a room.

Stones of wakeful nights when memories of people, events and regrets overtake your heart.

Stones of sins you are not certain are forgiven or forgotten. Stones of fear that you have no future save this place.

Receive the truth of the Gospel message.

God who brought again from the dead our Lord Jesus Christ has also rolled away the stones over your heart this Easter.

In Your spirit, hear now the grating sound as your stones are rolled away.

Take courage in your eternal future.

Your stones are rolled away in the Resurrection of Jesus Christ. Hallelujah! He is Risen! And so will you in Him as you accept Him as your Lord and Savior.

Amen.

Thanksgiving Day

Many are asking, "Who can show us any good?"
Let the light of Your face shine upon us, 0 Lord.
Psalm 4:6-7 (NIV)

Lord our God,

Let the light of Your face shine upon our nation in its celebration of the plenty and the freedom You granted and guided.

Bless us with the illumination to return to our ancestral pledge of "One nation under God".

Bless us with the enlightenment to include You in our public discourse.

Bless our military wherever they are deployed in defense against darkness.

Bless us with the motivation for greater works of charity that we might reflect You to those less fortunate in our midst.

Bless our nation, 0 Lord our God, with a holy light of revival and faithfulness to Your Son, Jesus Christ, for Whom we are most grateful this Thanksgiving Day.

Amen.

FAMILY

I KNEEL BEFORE THE FATHER FROM WHOM HIS WHOLE FAMILY IN HEAVEN IS DERIVED.

EPHESIANS 3:14

For Jake

For this reason a man will leave his father and mother and be united to his wife, and they will become one flesh.
Gen 2:24 (NIV).

Lord Jesus,

Thank You for the husband who waited for me at the altar of Epiphany Church on August 23, 1958. Your first miracle was performed at the marriage at Cana when You changed water into wine. The second miracle was our wedding when You turned two hearts into one union with You.

Thank You for the forty-seven years of that miracle. The good and the bad times; the joys and the sorrows; three sons; caring for and burying our parents; praying and traveling together in the kingdom of God.

Thank You for giving me a man of order and discipline, hard work and professional excellence, constant and dependable love all these years.

Thank You, Lord, for Jake.

Amen.

For Jake

But thou, O God, my Lord, deal on my behalf for Thy names' sake;
because Thy steadfast love is good, deliver me!
Psalm 109:21 (RSV)

Merciful Lord,

It is almost 2:30 and Jake will soon have his appointment about the lawsuit case.

Hear my prayer for my wonderful husband who has always worked hard and set such high standards for himself in his professional life.

Bless Jake, O God.

Give the attorney divinely inspired knowledge to aid in delivering Jake from this snare.

Protect Jake's morale and his faith; his heart and his health. Thank You, God, for Jake.

Amen.

12 June 87

For Jake

"It is not the healthy who need a doctor, but the sick".
Matt.9:12 (NIV)

Divine Physician, Lord Jesus,

Thank You for Jake's years of medical practice.

Thank You for calling him to the medical profession; for educating him in its knowledge and skill; for inspiring him to take the Hippocratic oath on June 17, 1960.

Your hand of blessing was upon the patients who came into the Radiation Therapy Department for Jake's care. In the pain and confusion and fear of their cancer diagnosis, they encountered a doctor with a gold Ichthus in the lapel of his white hospital coat and kindness in his blue eyes as he looked into their charts and into their hearts.

Thank You for Jake's recognition that You, Jesus, were the Primary Care Physician and he the secondary care provider for Your dear ones who suffered with cancer.

Thank You for his years of leadership of Discovery Weekend and his willingness to extend Your healing compassion and his energy to its participants.

Bless now the conclusion of his medical practice, even as You so generously blessed with grace those active years of the leather lunch box and the bow ties.

Thank You, Lord, for Jake.

Amen.

A Mother's Prayer (1979)

Lord Jesus,

I come before the throne of grace in intercession for the safely and health of my family. I ask You to protect each of my loved ones and me from violence, accidents, injury and illness, because Your love for them and for me is greater than even my own.

Your Word promises You send Your angels to protect us wherever we go and to steady us on our paths. The world and the hearts of men grow darker each day, but You are the Light of the World.

Send Your angels to protect each child, my husband and myself from the works of darkness that we might witness to Your truth.

We are Your people, Lord God. We are the sheep of Your pasture. Kind Shepherd, keep us safe and well. I ask these blessings knowing that all things are in Your power.

Thank You, Jesus.

Amen.

For my sons

Peace, peace to the far and to the near,
says the Lord; and I will heal him.
Is 57:19 (RSV)

Chris on USS America, sailing towards the Persian Gulf.
John building a skyscraper in Singapore.
Paul near at home, assembling his career.

Lord God,
   In Your great mercy, hear a mother's prayer for her sons. Grant to them the grace to reconcile their young lives with You.
   Protect Chris from harm. If he must fly into combat, be with him, O Savior. Sharpen his aviator's skills and mellow his heart to his Lord.
   Place Your healing touch upon John's rejection struggles and his spiritual needs. As he climbs girders and studies construction plans, build in his heart a sense of Your eternal Presence in his life.
   Grant to Paul Your healing mercy on his eyesight and his blood pressure as he prepares to exit our nest. Stabilize him and give him hope for the future plans You have for him.
   Thank You, Lord, for these fine men who are my sons and my fellow travelers in the Kingdom of God, be they far off or near.
      Amen.

For Chris

Heavenly Father,

Because of Your relationship with Your Son Jesus, I lift up to You my beloved son Chris ... "in whom I am well pleased". I ask Your blessing upon Chris. I pray for Your gift of his airline interview appointment to be established on or by his Birthday.

Grant this favor to him as an encouragement through a difficult time in his young and productive life. Open the window of Heaven and pour out Your Holy Spirit upon him as he approaches fatherhood, for You are the Eternal Father of all wisdom and strength.

Thank You, Father, for my son Chris who is such a joy to me and for Your Son Jesus Christ in whose Name I pray.

Amen.

For Chris Instrument Flying

You, O Lord, keep my lamp, burning;
my God turns my darkness into light.
Psalm 18:28(NIV)

Lord God Almighty,

At the creation of the world You commanded, "Let there be light" from the darkness over all the earth. And You sent Your Son, Jesus Christ, the Light of the World, to illuminate the hearts of mankind.

Replace, I beseech You, the darkness in Chris' mind about instrument flying. Transform that dark experience of practice under the hood into a victory for Chris. Enlighten his mind; sharpen his perception; improve his timing.

Only You, Heavenly Father, are able to enlighten this experience for Chris. I pray You do so in the Name of Your Son, Jesus Christ, who came to us that we might see the Light of Your Kingdom and be translated out of darkness into the Kingdom of Light. Thank You, Father.

Amen.

For Chris

A Pilot's Prayer

Lord God Almighty,

As I take off on the wings of the morning and fly to the far side of the sea, I commit my flight to Your loving protection and guidance. I rely upon Your hand to guide me through all maneuvers and missions. I depend not only upon technology and the plans of men, but upon Your right hand to uphold me in the exact use of them.

Because darkness is as light to You, I especially commit all night flying to Your care. All my flight hours are written in Your log book; all the days of my life ordained by You are written in Your book.

In Your mercy, bring me and my flying comrades safely through our flights on this tour. I pray for these blessings of Your protection in the Name of Your Son, Jesus Christ, who died for me that I might have eternal life. Thank You, Lord.

    Amen.

    Psalm 139:9-11

For Elise

Elise's Birthday

Lord God,

Today we are thankful for Elise's life. We are thankful You created this lovely young woman. You brought her into Chris' life as a wife and into our family as a daughter.

We are thankful for her parents who taught her their values, provided a fine home life and who love her. Bless Marlene and Chuck with a sense of satisfaction and fulfillment in this daughter You gave them. May their hearts be at peace.

Bless Elise, Lord, on this twenty-sixth birthday and on every day of her life.

Hear our prayer that she will grow each day in the knowledge of Your great love for her.

We pray these blessings for Elise in the Name of Your Son, the Lord Jesus Christ. Thank You, Lord, for Your grace in our dear Elise.

Amen.

For Elise Birthday 2 March 1988

... and they will call him Immanuel-which means, "God with us."
Mt. 1:23 (NLT)

Beautiful daughter, wife to my son, joy to my heart,

My prayer for you on your birthday is that you might always experience Immanuel-God with you-wherever you are and whatever your circumstances.

May Immanuel-God with you-guide you into excellence in your profession as a nurse.

May Immanuel-God with you-answer the secret desires of your heart.

May Immanuel-God with you-be with you and Chris in all mercy, safety, protection and health.

May Immanuel-God with you-reveal His perfect will to you and grant to you His strength in following it.

May Immanuel, the Lord Jesus Christ, bless each day of this new year in your life. He certainly blessed us with you

Amen.

For Elise

... 'The Teacher asks: Where is my guest room, where I may eat the Passover with my disciples?' He will show you a large upper room, furnished and ready.
Mark 14:14-15 (NIV)

Heavenly Father,

How we thank you for Elise's upper room heart. She has prepared a guest room in her heart and in her home for the Lord Jesus. It is a bright, warm and welcoming space of blessing to her family and all who enter there.

How we thank you for Elise's hospitality of heart and of home on our visits to Indianapolis.

How fitting, Lord, that she would prosper in a business designed to enhance the beauty and hospitality of women's homes with Southern Living at Home.

Thanks be to God for Elise's hospitality!

Amen.

Joshua Luke Hannemann
August 1992

Lord Jesus,

Thank You for the birth of Joshua.

Thank You for bringing him safely from creation into this life. Thank You for a new Hannemann generation, a new continuity of Your grace.

Surround the tiniest Hannemann, asleep in his crib, with Your holy angels, even as I surround him with my prayers. You were once an infant sleeping in a manger crib. May Joshua's life be lived in Your strength and guidance.

Hear my heart's prayer for Chris that he is fulfilled as a father to Joshua, in good relationship with his earthly father Jake and always close to his Heavenly Father, the Creator of Joshua and all life.

Thank You, Jesus, for the birth of Joshua.

Amen.

Joshua's Prayer

Lord Jesus,
    Be with me at the start of each day,
    Keep me alert in school and in play.
    Thank You for my books, TV and each toy,
    Thank You for being a nine year old boy.
    Give Mom blessings from Heaven above,
    To thank her for all her work and love.
    Always keep Daddy safe when he flies,
    With Holy Angels in Southwest skies.
    Watch over me day and night and then,
    I'll add "Thanks, Lord!" to my Amen.

For Joshua
Grandmom's Prayer

Lord Jesus,
    Thank you for Josh, my wonderful grandkid,
    Thank you for all he is and all he ever did.
    Thank you for the books we have read, the laughs we had,
    For making my grandmom's heart always proud and glad.
    For scaring me silly with ghosts and snakes,
    For eating burnt popcorn and chocolate shakes.
    Watch over him in safety at home or at school,
    Give him strength in baseball or in the pool.
    Bless Josh this Christmas 2002 with your holy joy,
    Remind him You once were also a ten year old boy.
    Help him know You and I love him and then,
    His happy grandmom will add her "Amen."

For John
3 Nov 83, in Yemen with The Peace Corps

Lord God,

Thank You for the fine son You gave me twenty-two years ago today. From that first day of his birth until now he is grown into manhood, John has been a special blessing to me.

I thank You for all the talents You have so richly granted to John. And I thank You even more that he has exerted the effort to develop and use these talents.

In Your mercy, bless John's Peace Corps tour with a sense of accomplishment and success. Keep him safe in a distant land among strangers. Let him know You are not a stranger and are ever close to help and guide him.

I ask these blessings for my son in the Name of Your Son, Jesus Christ. Thank You. Father.

Amen.

John's House

... we have a building from God, a house not made with hands,
eternal in the Heavens.
2 Cor. 5: 1 (RSV)

Your hands were the hands of a builder, engineer, artist.

A skyscraper in Singapore. An apartment complex in New York.
Embassy in Doha. Community Center in Yemen.

A final decade of building your house in Kezar Falls.

Doors hung. A floor laid. Roof shingled. Windows and skylights framed and set open to Maine light.

The orchard on a hill below and Mount Washington misty and majestic in the distance.

You are now in a house not made with your hands, but with God's, a house eternal.

His blueprint is of a different and divine design. Its materials not purchased from Home Depot.

You are fastened there by a secure nail, by Jesus Christ.

He built within you a house of faith.

Now all your windows look not out upon an orchard and mountain, but into the heart of God.

For John

Whether you are on earth or in Heaven,
Actively engaged in life or entering Eternity,
Whether in circumstances dire or divine,
Among artists and athletes or innumerable angels in festal array,
Working with imperfections and abrasions,
   or with spirits of just men made perfect,
Depressed and alone on one of your graysome days,
   or discussing the new Covenant with your Mediator,
Dining in a posh bistro with contemporaries,
   or hosting Jesus at the dinner table of your heart,
Struggling with the perfidy of relationships,
   or meeting the assembly of the first-born,
Negotiating the traffic and crowds of urbanity,
   or taking a taxi in the heavenly Jerusalem,
Wherever you are on earth or in heaven,
   Be blessed by the love of God and the prayers of your mother.
   Amen.
   Hebrews 12:22-24

For Paul

All the days ordained for me
Were written in your book,
before one of them came to be.
Psalm 139:16(NIV)

Blessed Lord Jesus,

What great joy to see this Scripture verse on my dear son Paul's birthday, and to realize You, the Alpha and the Omega, ordained all the days of his life, even before he was born. How I thank You for each chapter in Paul's life, each chapter written down by You in Your Book. Indeed, Your hand has been upon Paul in the good and in the bad times.

But Jesus ... each page has been a great blessing to me, so I want to thank You. In Your mercy, watch over Paul, especially in his long commute to work. Keep him safe. Keep him happy. Keep his heart always in You.

Thank You, Jesus.

Amen and Amen.

For Paul

Whoever does God's will is my brother and sister and mother.
Mark 3:35 (NIV)

Blessed Lord Jesus,

In Your great mercy, guide my dear son Paul in doing God's will. Speak to him in Your Holy Scripture; inform his sensibilities; inspire his energy and talents.

You see, Jesus, You are his Sacred Sibling, the one closest to him all his life.

Guide now Your brother Paul into the direction of his faith that You would have him follow.

In Your generosity of grace, grant to Paul the wisdom and the strength to answer Your call upon his life.

Thank You, Jesus, for Your brother and my son Paul.

Amen.

Most Valuable Paul

Then this Daniel became distinguished above
all the other presidents and satraps, because an
excellent spirit was in him;
Daniel 6:3(RSV)

Blessed Lord Jesus,

Thank You for the Spirit of Excellence in Paul.

Thank You for affirming his efforts in professional excellence with the Most Valuable Project Manager Award.

Thank You for the grace of such excellence that His loved ones consider him Most Valuable.

Most Valuable husband to Charlotte.

Most Valuable dad to Caleb and Nathan.

Most Valuable brother and friend in the Body of Christ.

Most Valuable son and brother in the Hannemann family.

Most Valuable traveling companion on the Kingdom journey.

In Your great mercy, bless him with peace to recognize The Spirit of Excellence, Your Promised Holy Spirit, is always with him that You might be glorified.

Thank You, Jesus.

Amen.

For Paul

How sweet are thy words to my taste,
sweeter than honey to my mouth.
Through thy precepts I get understanding;
therefore I hate every false way.
Psalm 119:103-104. (RSV)

Blessed Lord Jesus,

Thank you for the sweetness of your Scriptures. Thank you for speaking the sweetness of Redemption into the everyday struggles of our earthly lives. In your great mercy, inspire Paul's teaching on the Psalms. Guide his mind; enhance his articulation; quicken his courage. So guide and direct his teaching that each person attending the Sunday school class will leave the room with the sweet taste of You, Jesus, Sweet Redeemer. Thank you for Paul's faith and his willingness to teach your people.

Amen and Amen.

For Charlotte

... the time came for the baby to be born, and she gave birth to her firstborn, a son. She wrapped him in cloths and laid him in a manger
Luke 2:7 (NIV)

Dearest Lord Jesus,

Bless my dear daughter Charlotte in her motherhood. Fill her with joy and confidence.

Through Your Holy Presence, make each day of Caleb's care a day of satisfaction and of closeness to You.

How beautiful she is as a mother nursing her infant. Long silky brown hair and soft brown eyes. Like a painting of a Madonna.

Thus it must have resembled the scene when your mother nursed You at her breast. How we thank You for the Incarnation. You "thought it not robbery" to come down from Heaven and dwell among us in human flesh.

Nudge Your Holy Spirit to remind Charlotte of the Incarnation on those tough days of motherhood which will surely be. Remind her that You, also, have "been there" at Your mother's breast and are with her now. Where You are is perfect love.

Thank You, Jesus.

Amen.

For Charlotte

He (she) who loves a pure heart and whose speech is gracious will
have the king for his (her) friend).
Prov 22: 11 (NIV)

King Jesus,

Thank You for the gift of Charlotte to the Hannemann family.
Thank You for her love of a pure heart. To be with Charlotte is to feel
the heartbeat of her love for you in her intellect, energy, talents and
affections.

From this pure heart comes her gracious speech: words of kindness
and mercy, words of wisdom and encouragement, words of prayer and
faithfulness to You. The speech of grace from You, through Charlotte,
to all of us who love her.

Indeed, You are her Friend. How we thank You for Charlotte.

Amen.

For Charlotte

Dearest Lord Jesus,

March is almost here.

Charlotte's delivery approaches.

Bless these final weeks of her pregnancy with special peace.

In Your great love, make this an easy labor and delivery, a time of knowing You are present to love and support.

In the divine economy of your grace, make Nathan's birth a mystical healing of all the sadness that paralleled Charlotte's pregnancy. You alone make all things new, Lord. Make this birth a new time of healing for my dear Charlotte, my heart daughter. Grant to her an easy, physically strong and joyful post-partum time.

And, oh Dear Savior, prepare Caleb's little heart for Nathan. You see, Jesus, You alone have the wisdom, power and glory for accomplishing these gestures of grace for which I pray.

Thank You, Jesus.

Amen.

For Caleb John

July 2001

Heavenly Father,

Thank You for today's welcoming of Caleb John into the household of faith. Thank You for sealing him with Your Holy Spirit and making him as Christ's own forever.

In Your mercy, grant to him the grace of faithfulness and obedience to Your Holy Commandments. Grant to us, who love him, the courage to be witnesses to him.

We commend Caleb John's life to You, asking Your mercy and protection upon him. May he grow to his full stature in Christ Jesus, Your Beloved Son, who was once Himself a toddling lad among us and in whose Name we do pray.

Thank You, Father.

Amen.

Family

155

Caleb's Prayer

Dear Jesus,
    Watch over Your little boy,
    Be with every book and toy.

    Give to me Your holy grace,
    Shine upon my hands and face.

    Guard me, Jesus, if you please,
    From owies, bruises, scraped knees.

    Give me Your light as I grow,
    Closer to You from head to toe.

    You were once a little boy like me,
    Playing and running, chasing and free.

    Teach me to live in the better part,
    Where "the boy Jesus" lives in my heart.
        Amen. (Luke 2:43)

For Caleb

Lord God Almighty,

Today is my dear Caleb's second birthday. My grandmother-heart prays for a special blessing of grace for Caleb's life. I see, in memory, the brightness of his eyes, the intelligence and curiosity of expression, as Charlotte and Paul read to him from Holy Scripture and from little kid storybooks.

I pray, O Lord, for that brightness of Caleb's eyes to be present all through his life as he reads Scripture ... for the intelligence and the curiosity to be ever present, for Your Holy Spirit to inspire and teach Caleb in Your Holy Word. May the blessing of books be with my dear Caleb, and may the Bible be the most important book in his life.

Thank you, Lord.

Amen.

For Nathan

Dearest Lord Jesus,

Bless this dear lamb who waits in his mother's womb, just as you did all those centuries ago. It has been a rough pregnancy for his mom, just as it was for your young mom.

The times and traditions, the era and its problems, the manger and the hospital technology are different. The miracle of creation of a life is the same. The miracle of Nathan's life is Your gift.

How we thank You, Jesus, for Nathan. In these remaining weeks, watch over him in precious care, for he is a lamb of Your own shepherding, en route to our hearts and his mother's arms.

Amen.

For Nathan James

Heavenly Father,

How we rejoice this day to bring Nathan James before you for Baptism into the death of Jesus Christ and into the power of His Resurrection.

Thank You for bringing Nathan James into the new life of grace. In Your great mercy, watch over him each day that he may continue as Christ's own forever. Direct his steps in Your holy ways. Bless him with a discerning heart and the courage to choose life in You.

By the power of Your Holy Spirit, strengthen our precious child Nathan James for service to Your own precious Son, Jesus Christ, in whose Name we pray.

Amen.

For Nathan

Nathan said to David, "You are the man."
2 Sam 12:7 (RSV)

Almighty God,

Watch over our dear Nathan's childhood and maturity into the manhood You planned for him in creation.

Guide his physical and spiritual growth with the strength only You can provide in Your Comforter.

The era, the generation, the condition of men's hearts into which Nathan was born are covered with darkness and godlessness. Be generous in grace to fill his heart with passion for bringing the souls of his contemporaries into the Kingdom.

Aptly named for the prophet who did not cower from Your calling, give to Nathan the courage to call out his generation that You might be glorified.

Thank You for Nathan.

Amen.

For Melanie

I am a rose of Sharon
A lily of the valley
As a lily among brambles,
So is my love among maidens.
Song 2:1-2 (RSV)

Dearest Lord Jesus,

Your name is "Lily of the Valley", because You bloom in the valley, in the dark and low times of our lives.

In Your great mercy, bloom in Melanie's heart during this valley she must travel through. It is a difficult time, a chastening time, a time of reflection and growth.

Bloom for her, Dear Jesus.

Let her know You love her, You are for her, You stand by her.

And so do I.

Only Your grace, Jesus, can work such strength and comfort.

Thank You for my dear Melanie and for our years of friendship and mutual support in our journey towards You.

Be with her now, Dear Jesus, our Friend and Savior, our Healer and our Hope, our Lily of the Valley.

Amen.

For Melanie

Then He rose and rebuked the winds and the sea;
and there was a great calm.
Matt. 8:26(RSV)

Dearest Lord Jesus,

We entrust to You a most precious passenger who begins her voyage with cancer today, 1 July 1999.

Whether it will be a rough or a calm sea is unknown to us.

Whether there will be storms and hurricanes, fair or chill winds we cannot predict.

You, Lord, have the outcome, the harbor in Your hands. Bless her as she sails; be her compass in troubling times; be her anchor when she needs safe mooring.

In Your great mercy, make of this voyage an adventure in healing, a miracle of Your grace and power.

Jesus, You are the ultimate doctor, the Great Physician who heals. Be thus for Melanie, Dear Lord.

Thank You for Melanie and for her courage in setting out to sea.

Amen.

For Melanie

May the faith and love that are in Christ Jesus overflow for you in your pregnancy.

May you be well physically; strong, healthy, energetic of body, mind and heart.

May your sense of yourself as a woman, your womanliness, be blessed and enhanced.

May He, who was carried in a pregnancy and born in a delivery, be apparent to you each day in your certainty of his love and care.

May God be gracious to you that no cancer complications accompany this pregnancy. May you know He honors you because you honored His creation by agreeing to carry your baby to term.

This is my prayer for you, Melanie, my dearest daughter of the heart.

May every word of this prayer and every grace of God be real to you.

Amen.
Eph.3:16-17

For Ryan

Dearest Lord Jesus,

Bless this dear little one who is to be born today. Place Your hand of grace and of favor upon his birth. Bless his tiny presence among us.

Consecrate him unto Yourself that he would grow into a fine and healthy lad and a strong and productive man of God. By the miracle of Your grace, make him the best-ever of the McKeans. Nurture and direct his life that he will be great joy to his Mom.

We are in awe, Lord, of a new life. All of Your creation is changed and better for this little one's appearance today.

Thank You, Jesus, for his life.

Amen.

For Ryan

Blessed Lord Jesus,

Thank You for Ryan's Baptism. Thank You for welcoming him into the household of faith.

As You were presented in the temple as an infant, we present Ryan to You in the temple of our hearts. In Your generosity of grace, consecrate his life to love and serve You. Grant to us who love him the courage to be witnesses to him.

Ryan is so recently come from You that he reminds us of You and fills our hearts with reverence for Your creation. Send Your holy angels to watch over him ... always ... all ways. Thank You, Lord.

Amen.

For Ryan

When we cry, "Abba! Fatherl", it is the Spirit himself bearing witness
with our spirit that we are children of God.
Rom 8:15-16(RSV)

Abba, Daddy,

Bless Your dear Ryan with the knowledge of You as his father. Watch
over and protect him as he grows into the man You created Him to be.
A man of faith and truth; a man of Scripture and focus; a Godly man
to his generation.

Mercifully guard and refresh with grace the well-springs of his heart
that he might experience life as a child of God and an heir to Your
promises.

Be Ryan's constant and paternal encourager in his years of school
and growing up; education and career; marriage and family as a father
himself.

We entrust Ryan to your Divine Fatherhood.

Place in his little boy's heart the passion for Your own Son, the Lord
Jesus Christ in whose Name we pray. Thank You, Father.

Amen.

Grandmother's Blessing

And the child grew and became strong, filled with wisdom;
and the favor of God was upon him.
Luke 2:40(RSV)

May you grow tall as a man as did Jesus.

May you grow strong in body, in mind and in heart as did Jesus.

May all your strength be in knowing He is always beside you, a friend invisible to others, always visible in your heart and mind.

May you accept His friendship because He was once a boy of your age. He created you and He knows and loves you as no one ever can.

May your growing be filled with wisdom at every age, choice and problem.

His boyhood was different in time and place from yours now. No TV, movies, computer, soccer, baseball, swimming, PSP, bikes, popcorn, ice cream and soda.

But as He grew, the favor of God was upon him.

May you be blessed by knowing the favor of God is upon you in believing in Jesus.

May you always remember His favor upon you as you grow to manliness in Him. May you be blessed by your grandmother's prayers for you, Joshua, Caleb, Nathan and Ryan.

Amen.

For Margaret Mary Elliott Holmberg

In his hand is the life of
every living creature,
and the breath of all mankind.
Job 12:10(NIV)

HOLY SPIRIT OF GOD ..... BREATH OF LIFE,
How we thank You for the life of Margaret.

Thank You for the children she bore and the mothering of them through all the troubles and triumphs of life.

Thank You for the quality of her heart in family relationships and in friendships. It was of such quality that we who harbored in her love were forever changed by welcoming shelter and strength to continue on.

Thank You for her valiant struggle to breathe and still be the Margo of the Woolies, the Margo of the Giggies, the Margo of the Giggles.

Thank You that her struggle is over. Her lungs are now filled with the breath of God in the eternal place where there is no pain, nor sorrow, nor tears, but only the joy of Irish eyes smiling.

Certain we shall see her again, we commend her to Your care, asking that the grace of Your Holy Breath keep us in our sorrow, close to the Lord Jesus Christ, in whose Name we pray.

Amen.

13 March 06

For Ann Lutrede Elliott Herrick

How beautiful you are, my darling!
How beautiful!
Your eyes are soft like doves.
Song of Solomon 4:1 (NLT)

Almighty God,

Thank You for the life of Ann.

Indeed, how beautiful she was.

A woman of spiritual beauty in faith and in devotion to Your church. Your people in the church were as precious to her as they are to You. A woman of family beauty. Half a century of marriage, four children, seven grandchildren; holidays and trips and celebrations, always remembering and providing beautiful events and gifts.

A woman of hospitality in her beautifully appointed home, always set forth with the unique Ann touch of excellent taste. A woman of extraordinary physical beauty in her elegant clothing and appearance.

Lord God, Your beloved Ann and our beloved Ann.

We shall not see again such beauty of face and form, faith and friendship until she greets us in eternity where You called to her, "Rise up, my beloved, my fair one , and come away" (Song 2:10).

Come away to a Heaven we can only glimpse in our grief.

Until such time of reunion, we commend her to Your mercy in Your Son, the Lord Jesus Christ, whom her soul loves and in whose Name we pray.

Amen.

20 January 2007

For John Paul Elliott, Jr.

A friend loves at all times,
and a brother is born for adversity.
Proverbs 17:17(RSV)

Heavenly Father,
    Thank You for my brother Jack.
    Thank You for his leadership of the
    Fab Four Elliotts and his concern for the
        well-being of his sisters.
    Thank You for his modeling leadership
        of his own family, respect for his dear wife
    Betty and care for his children, grandchildren
    and great-grand-children.

                A man of loyalty to friends.
                An engineer of skill and ingenuity.
                A reader of books and lover of music.
                A humorist of extraordinary wit.
                A conversationalist of ideas and dreams.

Indeed, a brother born of adversity in help
        and guidance through the time of caring for our
        own parents and the loss of our sisters.
In Your great mercy, bless him with the
        knowledge of Your Presence in his life and of
Your love for him and my love for him.
Thank You for my brother Jack.
    Amen.

CHURCH

IN HIM THE
WHOLE
BUILDING IS
JOINED
TOGETHER
AND RISES TO
BECOME A HOLY
TEMPLE
IN THE LORD.

EPHESIANS 2:21

Come, Holy Spirit, upon the church named in Your honor that You might work in the hearts and in the lives of the people of God.

Come, Spirit of God, as joy in our worship.

Come, Spirit of Christ, as our light in sharing the Redemption of our Lord and Savior, Jesus Christ.

Come, Power of the Highest, as our flame of compassion for the unredeemed, the addicted, the sick, the lonely, the dying and the bereaved.

Come, Spirit of Truth, as our Teacher of the mind of God revealed in Holy Scripture.

Come, Spirit of Wisdom and Understanding, as our liaison to the priests and people of the Diocese of Maine, that we might be brothers and sisters in the household of faith.

Come, Holy Spirit, as a blessing upon our Bishop Edward who has established our assembly.

Spirit of Holiness. Spirit of Prayer. Excellent Spirit. Come, Holy Spirit, upon our church.

Amen.

The Church of the Holy Spirit Portland, Maine

The Church of the Holy Spirit

First Service of the Reverend James C. King,
July 1990, Portland, ME.

Almighty God,

Thank You for Father Jim and his new ministry to the Church of
the Holy Spirit.

Thank You for placing the plummet in his hands.

Thank You for his heart that does not disdain the day of small
beginnings.

Bless Father Jim in this small beginning which is The Church of the
Holy Spirit.

Be generous in grace to him, to his dear wife and family and to us,
his congregants, for increased faithfulness and holy purpose.

In Your great love for Father Jim and for Your church, guide and
inspire his pastorate in glorifying Your Son, Jesus Christ, in whose
Name we pray.

Amen.

Zec 4:10

Covenant Prayer
The Church of the Holy Spirit

Heavenly Father,

We ask Your blessing upon each one who has signed the Covenant of the Church of the Holy Spirit. How we rejoice today in welcoming them all into the covenant of our congregation, for it is symbolic of our covenant with You and Your eternal faithfulness to us.

Bid Your Holy Spirit strengthen the different gifts You have given to new members of this covenant. In Your great love, help them find Your will in the expression of their particular gifts and grace. Keep our hearts ever humble and hospitable in including these brothers and sisters in our fellowship with one another and with You.

Our fondest desire is that their joy in Jesus Christ may be complete, and we might participate with them in its completion. We pray they might always remain in the friendship and love of Your Son, the Lord Jesus Christ, in whose name we pray for each new member.

Amen.

Deut. 7:9

Diocesan Day of Prayer
3 Nov 1990

Send forth your light and your truth; let them guide me;
let them bring me to your holy mountain, to the place where you dwell.
Psalm 43:3 (NIV)

A Prayer for You

May the Lord God send out His light, the Light of Christ, to you when you pray.

May God fill you with the Holy Spirit, the Spirit of Truth, in finding His will for your life.

May God's light and truth lead you to the holy hill of Calvary where you will experience forgiveness and healing at the foot of the Cross.

May you carry the redemptive message of the Cross to all persons you encounter.

May you go from this Prayer Workshop happy in Christ and filled with His joy.

May you experience God's blessing and my thankfulness for our time together, seeking more of Him through prayer journal writing. In the Name of Jesus Christ, I ask these blessings for you.

Amen.

Altar Guild Prayer

Let the favor of the Lord our God be upon us,
and establish Thou the work of our hands upon us,
Yea, the work of our hands, establish Thou it.
Psalm 90:17 (RSV)

Almighty God,

In Your love for the church, let Your favor be upon us in our Altar Guild work. Through the power of Your Holy Spirit, transform our efforts into a blessing of holy hospitality to all who worship in our parishes. Grant to us efficiency, increased faithfulness and cheerfulness in all our endeavors. Draw us closer to You and to one another in our service.

We pray that You would establish the work of our hands as we set the Holy Table for the Supper of Your Son, the Lord Jesus Christ, in whose name we pray.

Thank You, Lord God, for the gift of this service.

Amen.

For Father Jim King

May you know anew each day that God carries your soul in His arms just as you have carried Jesse, Jason and Katie in yours.

May you be at peace with the working of God in your soul. May your "father places" be healed: your relationship with your earthly father, with your Divine Father in Heaven, and with your tasks and cares as The Reverend Father Jim King.

May the decisions, discouragements and distractions of your pastorate be always protected in the Father's care for you.

May you awaken each morning with the certainty that your Father God will never snuff nor lessen the flame of Christ in you.

May you be so carried in His arms.

Amen.

Deut.33:27

For Bishop Craig Bates

Dearest Lord Jesus,

Be merciful to post holy angels over Bishop Craig's car on the long snow filled drive to Maine. Keep him in all safety, alert and strangely refreshed.

Your Gospel tells us the angels came and ministered to You.

We ask for the same generous ministry for our dear Bishop on this journey.

As the Eternal Bishop of our souls, You understand the cares of our Diocesan Bishop in preparing us all for an eternal appointment with You. Help him prepare his message to us, and help us to receive it.

Watch over the Bates home and his loved ones in his absence. Thank You, Lord, for Bishop Craig and Cathy and all their efforts for You and Your people in Your church.

Amen.

Psalm 91:11.

For Bishop Craig Bates

Enable Your servant Bishop Craig to hear You saying, "Come away, my beloved."

Through the power of Your Holy Spirit, give him the strength to come away from the pressures and people, the plans and pomp of office, the directions and decisions, to quiet fellowship with You.

In Your great love for him, refresh his energy and rekindle his joy.

Be generous in grace that he would hear Your calling him into Your Presence where he can be refreshed and at peace as Your beloved and our Bishop.

Amen.

Songs 2:10

Andrew Hearts

(Dedicated to Bishop Craig Bates, a brother of the Andrew heart)

Almighty God,

In Your great mercy, grant to us Andrew hearts that we might be listeners and learners of the Lamb of God.

Strengthen our wills to go to our contemporaries with the news, "We have found the Messiah."

Strengthen our energies to introduce them to Jesus, as Andrew did for Simon Peter.

Bid Your Holy Spirit replace our temerity with courage for evangelizing our present moment in history. We long to join You in transforming these perilous times with Your Light.

Illuminate our hearts and our lives with the holy purpose for sharing the Light of the World, Your Son Jesus Christ in whose name we pray.

Amen.

John 1:40-42

For Bishop Edward Chalfant

Dearest Lord Jesus,

All thanks to You for Bishop Edward's Ordination Anniversary on this date. Bless his travel today and his meeting, undertaken for You in shepherding Your church. Refresh him with Your Holy Presence.

Return to him the joy and the expectation of that December 18 when he committed himself to the priesthood.

As he promised to nourish Your people from the riches of Your grace and strengthen them to glorify God in this life and in the life to come, nourish and strengthen Bishop Edward for these tasks as only You can.

Thank You, Lord Jesus, for calling Bishop Edward to the priesthood and thus blessing us all with Your grace.

Amen.

18 Dec 1990

For Bishop Edward Chalfant

Spirit of Prayer,

Regard the prayers of Bishop Edward with all tenderness. Hear these prayers from his manly heart for God. Swiftly carry them to the throne of grace. Encourage and enrich his prayer time for his loved ones, his flock and himself. In his career of much public praying, bless and illuminate his prayers. Be always present in the secret room of his heart where the Father hears in secret.

Gentle Spirit, carry Bishop Edward's prayers in all haste and care. Fill his heart spaces, vacated by the journey of his intercessions to Heaven, with the joy only a heart of love can experience that we who love him might see more clearly the Lord Jesus Christ whose Sweet Spirit You are.

Come, Holy Spirit. Regard Edward's prayers.

Amen.

Mt. 6:6

For Bishop Edward Chalfant

Dearest Lord Jesus, Living Water,

Be merciful to keep the heart of Your friend Bishop Edward.

May rivers of Your grace and Your truth always flow from him. Grant to him such faith that all the thirst of his life and of his work might be quenched in the astonishment of Your love for him.

So refresh Bishop Edward in his own thirst for You that all who seek him as Bishop, as friend and as brother will be blessed by rivers of You, Jesus, flowing from his heart.

Thank You, Jesus, for Edward.

Amen.

John 7:37-38

The Church of the Holy Spirit, Kigali, Rwanda

Almighty God,

All praise to You, our Creator.

The people of the Church of the Holy Spirit, Portland, Maine, ask Your blessings upon the faithful people of The Church of the Holy Spirit, Kigali, Rwanda.

Mercifully be present to them as strength in their struggle, supply in their needs and answers to their prayers.

Be present to them in the comfort and encouragement of Your Holy Spirit.

Across the distance of miles and of cultures, they are brothers and sisters to us in the household of God.

Bid Your Holy Spirit inspire both churches as they join together and grow into a holy temple in the Lord.

Guide our dear friend and brother, Bishop Emmanuel, in caring for his people, as would the Eternal Bishop of their souls, the Lord Jesus.

We pray You will hold our association in shared and sacred faithfulness to Your Son, the Lord Jesus Christ, in whose Name we pray. Thank You, Father.

Amen.

Ephesians 2:19-22

For Pastor Ed and Ruth Bailey

Lord Jesus,

Thank You for my spiritual parents, Ruth and Ed.

Thank You for their bringing me into the fullness of the Spirit. Thank You for their nourishing in me the love of Scripture.

Thank You for their modeling the discipline and the obedience of faith.

Thank You for their treasured teaching of prayer based upon the Word of God. Thank You for their readiness to counsel, to comfort and to pray for me.

Thank You for their ministering the love of Christ to my husband and sons.

Thank You for their teaching me by precept to come first to You for direction in all areas of my life.

Always faithful to You.

Always willing to serve and uphold.

Always pointing perspective towards eternal fellowship with you. In Your generosity of grace, always bless and sustain Ed and Ruth. Always. All ways. Thank You, Lord Jesus.

Amen.

Hebrews 4:16

For Ruth Bailey

Lord Jesus,

Thank You for Ruth's befriending me in the Community of the Living Word. Thank you for our friendship in studying Scriptures, praying for each other, sharing our womanly hearts.

Thank You for her encouragement to hear Your voice, believe You and follow Your commands.

Thank You for her calling me from friendship with the world to friendship with You. Even now in memory, I hear her voice ... "there is a friend who sticks closer than a brother (Prov 18:24) and that friend is Jesus."

Thank You for Ruth's friendship.

Now separated by time and by miles as we may be, Your Holy Presence is still in our friendship.

Hear my prayer to bless and strengthen Ruth as God's friend and as mine.

Thank You, Lord.

    Amen.

    Jas. 2:23

The Root Cellar

I tell you, lift up your eyes, and see how the fields
are already white for harvest
John 4:35 (RSV)

Heavenly Father,

All praise to You for the Root Cellar.

Thank You for the staff and volunteers who go into the fields white with harvesting souls.

In Your mercy, stretch out Your hand to strengthen each dear one who labors there.

Refresh them with Your Holy Spirit who energizes all service.

Bid Your holy angels protect their souls and physical safety.

May all who enter 94 Washington Avenue perceive Your anointing on the building and Your Holy Presence in this place.

Hear our prayer in the Name of Your Son, Jesus Christ, who regarded even a cup of water to a little one as to Him for Your glory.

Amen.

Nursing Home Thirst

The woman said to him, "Sir, give me this water that
I may not thirst, nor come here to draw."
John 4:15 (RSV)

Blessed Jesus,

We believe You are the Living Water of eternal life. We are thirsty,
all of us, for more of You.

We have lost loved ones to death, divorce, distance of miles. We have
physical pain. We have fear. We have loneliness, confusion, even doubt
and disbelief.

We drink of You, Jesus. We open our souls, hearts and minds to
swallow unto ourselves Your Living Water.

We would have only You, Jesus, to satisfy us.

We give our hearts to You for flooding, so that out of our hearts may
flow streams of Living Water for the other residents and the staff of this
nursing home. Thank You, Lord.

Amen.

Our Prayer For You

Almighty God,

Bless this dear one to whom we give our prayer card.

Hear the cry of the heart for healing of body, peace of mind and joy in relationship with You.

O, God, You are the master of all time. In Your great love for this dear one, make the time of residence at Gorham House a time of happiness and closeness to You, a time of realizing, "Surely the Lord is in this place, and I did not know it" (Gen 28: 16, RSV).

Strengthen bodies, heal memories, restore relationships, Lord God.

Hear the special needs known privately to You and to this dear one who has worshiped with us today.

Bring the joy of Your presence into every room, hall and niche of Gorham House.

Bring new attitudes, new dreams and new hopes.

Hear our prayer, O God, for these dear friends, for we pray for them in the name of the One who makes all things new, Your Son Jesus Christ.

Amen.

The Church of the Holy Spirit

For The Church of the Holy Spirit

Restore our fortunes, O Lord,
like the watercourses in the Negeb!
Psalm 126:4 (RSV)

Lord God, Most Holy of Watercourses,

Mercifully restore the energy and the mission of The Church of the Holy Spirit.

Restore our ability to understand and follow Your words in Holy Scripture.

Restore our motivation to evangelize our contemporaries with the message of Your salvation.

Restore to us the hope for healing and commitment in fellowship.

Restore to us the passion for our first love, Jesus, our Blessed Hope.

You alone, O God, are the source of the wholeness our souls thirst after during dry times of struggle and sorrow.

Refresh us with the winter rains of Your favor that out of our hearts and our congregation may flow rivers of Living Water, Your Son, Jesus Christ in whose Name we pray.

Thank You, Lord.

Amen.

About the Author

Judith Hannemann is a prayerwright, crafting the mercy of God into words for her loved ones. The prayers of this volume are her gift of encouragement. Prayers for cancer patients resulted from Discovery Weekend, a seminar for cancer patients and their families, which she facilitates with her husband. She lives in Maine where she teaches English at the University of Southern Maine.

Photo by Stewart Smith

About the Illustrator

Christine Simoneau Hales is a painter, iconographer, and Art Therapist. She currently lives in the Hudson Valley with her photographer husband, Mick Hales.

They are both active in the Christian Healing Prayer Ministry and use their art wherever possible to further God's Kingdom.

Christine gives workshops and retreats On "Praying with Icons", teaches icon writing, and exhibits the icons nationally.

For more information on her work, or to contact her: www.Halesart. com or email: chales@halesartcom.

Photo by Mick Hales

Printed in the United States
202840BV00003B/340-417/P